STRATEGIES FOR IDENTIFYING WORDS

STRATEGIES FOR IDENTIFYING WORDS

**A Workbook
for Teachers and
Those Preparing to Teach**

SECOND EDITION

Dolores Durkin
University of Illinois

Allyn and Bacon, Inc.
Boston, London, Sydney, Toronto

Library of Congress Cataloging in Publication Data

Durkin, Dolores.
 Strategies for identifying words.

 Includes bibliographical references and index.
 1. Reading. 2. Word recognition. 3. Children—Language.
I. Title.
LB1050.D83   1981   372.4'144   80–26364
ISBN 0–205–07229–1

Printed in the United States of America

12 13 14 15 16 17   93 94 95 96 97 98

Series Editor: Margaret Quinlin
Production Editors: Joanne Dauksewicz
                     Rowena Dores

To the memory of my brother Bill

CONTENTS

PREFACE

Much to cover and too little time to cover it is a real problem for instructors of reading methodology courses. Not only must their students learn what to teach, they must also learn how to teach it to children. The dilemma, then, is: How can a single course cover both the *what* and the *how* for a sizable number of topics? One solution is to have students learn some of the essential content on their own; the course itself can then deal with how to teach it to children.

This book was written to contribute to such a solution, for it allows for independent learning of content concerned with word identification. Because the specific goal is to cover what children need to know in order to figure out unfamiliar words without the help of a more able reader or a dictionary, *Strategies for Identifying Words* focuses on the four kinds of cues that make independent identifications possible: syntactic, semantic, phonic, and structural. Students in reading methodology courses can monitor their own progress in mastering the content by taking the tests that appear intermittently. The Glossary (Appendix B) will also be of help to anyone who wants to study or review important terminology.

With its format, *Strategies for Identifying Words* can be used independently not only by students enrolled in a course but also by individual teachers who feel unsure of what to teach to help children cope with unknown words. With the limited focus, this workbook should also be useful for minicourses sponsored by colleges and universities and by school systems themselves.

Regardless of who uses it, *Strategies for Identifying Words* is meant to be studied rather than skimmed. Such study should result in knowledge and security, which, in turn, will allow for instruction that is both correct and productive for reading.

Dolores Durkin

INTRODUCTION

In recent years, scholars from a variety of disciplines have been giving an unprecedented amount of attention to reading comprehension. Since comprehending is the very essence of reading, one can only say, "It's about time!"

To comprehend connected text (the typical concern of readers), children must know the individual words that make up the phrase, sentence, or more. Consequently, helping them acquire the ability to identify unknown words is one major responsibility for their teachers.

■ ■ Ways to Identify Words

Words that are unfamiliar in their written form can be identified in various ways. If a more able reader is nearby, asking, "What does this word say?" may be all that's needed. Or if a dictionary is close at hand, consulting that should get the job done. The problem with these two sources of help is that they are not always available. Since they are not, children must have the information and skills that will enable them to solve word problems on their own. Fostering independence (the concern of this book) involves teaching children how to use three different kinds of cues. (A *cue* is a signal or hint that prompts a response.) The three are referred to as contextual, grapho-phonic, and structural cues.

Contextual Cues

For anyone attempting to identify a word, one helpful cue is the verbal context in which it is found. For that reason, this type of help is called a *contextual cue*. The source of contextual cues is usually thought of as being a sentence—specifically, the one in which the unfamiliar word is embedded. However, it can be either less or more than that.

Contextual cues are the first type of help dealt with in this book because they are what children should look to initially whenever they encounter an unfamiliar or forgotten word. If glass is unknown, for example, and it is in the sentence The glass on that picture needs to be cleaned, a reader should im-

3

mediately consider the eight known words to see what they suggest about the unknown one. Systematic consideration of known words to figure out an unknown word is the subject of Chapter 2, "Use of Context to Identify Words."

Graphophonic Cues

Because English has an alphabetic writing system, a second source of help with unknown words is rooted in the connection between a word's spelling and its pronunciation. Using the connection, readers can work out the identity of words like <u>fin</u>, <u>shade</u>, and <u>broom</u> even if they are in a context that offers minimal help. Using spellings to achieve pronunciations is taking advantage of *graphophonic cues* (*grapho* = letter, *phonic* = sound). What is taught to help children use those cues to identify a word constitutes the content of phonics instruction, which is the subject of Chapter 3.

Even when phonics instruction is thorough, graphophonic cues offer only incomplete help if a word has an irregular spelling (that is, shows a less than perfect correspondence between the way it is spelled and the way it is pronounced). However, as the chapter on phonics will explain, trying out different sounds (especially for vowels) will often yield correct identifications, particularly when contextual help is used, too. In other instances, knowing how to pronounce one irregularly spelled word (e.g., <u>could</u>, <u>shoe</u>) will help achieve the identification of another (e.g., <u>should</u>, <u>canoe</u>). In still other cases (e.g., <u>colonel</u>, <u>indict</u>, <u>chamois</u>), irregularly spelled words have to be identified by teachers or dictionaries. Direct identifications by teachers are required even for some regularly spelled words when children are still in the process of acquiring proficiency in using graphophonic cues.

To sum up, direct identifications by teachers (sometimes referred to as whole word methodology) are fairly common at the beginning but become much less frequent as children gradually learn to use spellings to achieve identifications on their own.

Structural Cues

Well-taught children can use a word's spelling to learn about its pronunciation and to arrive at an understanding of its structure. Understanding a word's structure is important for reading because it assists not only with the word's pronunciation but also with its meaning. To illustrate, the spellings of such words as <u>unclean</u>, <u>pointless</u>, and <u>cooked</u> suggest their structure is made up of a root plus an affix. The spellings further suggest not only how to pronounce the words but also how the affixes <u>un-</u>, <u>-less</u>, and <u>-ed</u> affect the meaning of the roots <u>clean</u>, <u>point</u>, and <u>cook</u>.

Spellings that provide information about structure are called *structural cues.* They are dealt with in Chapter 4.

■ ■ Using Cues

Although each of the three types of cues is considered in a separate chapter, it is important to recognize at the outset that proficient reading is characterized by a use of all three almost simultaneously. Thus, if good readers first encountered <u>tines</u> in the sentence <u>Use the tines to prick the pie</u>, they would be likely to consider the contextual, graphophonic, and structural cues in a way that came close to being one, multidimensional consideration. To be noted, too, is that once children know about the three sources of help, they should be encouraged to use them in their own way. The strategy any one child *will* use depends on that child, on the word causing problems, on the context in which it happens to be embedded, on the child's previous attempts to identify other unfamiliar words, and on the words the child knows. What counts in the end is that the unknown word *is* identified. The purpose of this book is to help you become aware of what needs to be taught so that both correct and swift identifications will be the rule for children, not the exception.

■ ■ Using This Book

To maximize the likelihood that the purpose of this book will be realized, a few suggestions will be made right away. One is that you read the chapters carefully and that you slow down, ponder, and study whenever you find something that seems complicated or is new to you. Because teaching children requires the ability to put into words what needs to be taught, another suggestion is that you memorize some of the material. Definitions, for example, should be committed to memory; so, too, should something like the spelling generalizations in the chapter dealing with structural cues. These suggestions are made because understanding, combined with memorization, eliminates the need to run to teaching manuals "just to check." In fact, it is to get you away from those manuals and to encourage you to stand on your own two professional feet that this book was written. If you are not a freer, more independent instructor as a result of studying its contents, the book will not have achieved its central goal.

To foster the attainment of that goal, your written responses will be requested from time to time. Complying should promote greater involvement with the material. A comparison of responses with the Answer Key also provides a self-check on comprehension. (To facilitate checking, you may want to tear out the Answer Key.)

TESTING

In the end, you are the one who must decide whether your study techniques are working. To learn if they worked for this brief, introductory chapter, let's see whether you can now define the following terms, all of which are concerned with a reader's efforts to identify unfamiliar words.

1. *Graphophonic cues* are ___________________________________

____

2. *Structural cues* are ___________________________________

____

3. *Contextual cues* are ___________________________________

____

4. A *cue* is ___________________________________

____

Please check your definitions with those in the Answer Key at the back of the book. If the check reveals incorrect or inadequate definitions, or if it was difficult to compose one or more of them, you will probably want to read more carefully.

Alphabetic writing system was referred to in this chapter and in the answer to the first question. Let's see, therefore, if you can complete the following.

An *alphabetic writing system* is ________________________

____

Again, please check what you wrote with the Answer Key.

■ ■ A Final Comment

To be remembered is that this book was written for teachers, not children. Its method of presenting content, therefore, is not to be viewed as a model for teaching the same content to children. Inevitably, they need a slower pace, a generous number of illustrations, frequent reviews, and many opportunities to apply what they are learning.

While knowing the content presented in this book should help teachers to instruct children in how to identify unfamiliar words, it cannot guarantee superior instruction; for that is the product of much more than just knowledge. Nonetheless, it goes without saying that one cannot teach what one does not know. In fact, one cannot teach what one does not know *well.* That is why you have been urged to read this book carefully, to reread certain parts whenever that seems necessary, and to respond in writing to all the self-evaluation exercises. Checking the Answer Key for each exercise is also recommended, not only because it will allow you to monitor your own comprehension, but also because the Answer Key sometimes provides additional information about the topic under consideration.

USE OF CONTEXT TO IDENTIFY WORDS

Although classroom chalkboards sometimes display words arranged in lists, everyday reading is rarely concerned with single, isolated words. Instead, it is usualiy done to comprehend connected text that may be as limited as a phrase or as extensive as a book. Some type of verbal context, therefore, is commonly available to help whenever readers come across new or forgotten words.

Putting the spotlight on connected text is not meant to deny the need for teachers to attend to individual words. Whenever a new one occurs, and whenever an old one is causing problems, children should be helped to scrutinize it with care. It still must be said, nonetheless, that more classroom time ought to go to connected text than is now typical, especially at the primary-grade level.

When children *are* given frequent opportunities to deal with connected text, they are at the same time being given the chance to use words they know to help them identify those they don't know. What can be done to teach children how to use contexts for that purpose is the concern of this chapter.

Even though that *is* the concern, it should be remembered that what is *not* on a page also assists a reader. Here I have in mind two closely related kinds of help that are in the reader's head: (a) background knowledge and (b) oral vocabulary. In this case, your own experiences verify that the more you know about a topic—including the vocabulary associated with it—the easier it is to cope not only with the whole of a text but also with the individual words that compose it.

■ ■ Types of Contexts

On the page, two kinds of contextual help exist. The first we'll call general; the second, local.

The *general* context is the selection (article, story, paragraph) in which the unfamiliar word is found. General contexts are helpful with identifications because their theme, or content, establishes expectations. An article about swimming, for instance, leads a reader to expect, thus to predict, words like water, shallow, pool, stroke, and practice. With a story, sources of general contextual help are its setting, its particular types of characters, and the events that constitute the plot.

Local contexts are more limited, for they are the particular sentences in which unknown words are embedded. In an article about swimming, an unknown word like <u>practice</u> might be in the local context <u>It takes practice to be a good swimmer.</u> In a story, the unknown word <u>angry</u> might initially be found in a local context such as <u>When John saw what the dog had done, he became angry.</u>

Even though local contexts are the focus of this chapter, the other sources of help for identifying words (background knowledge, listening and speaking vocabularies, general context) should not be overlooked either in your thoughts or in the instructional program that you establish to teach children to read both skillfully and independently.

TESTING

To see whether you can independently define some terms, please complete the following sentences.

1. A *general context* is ____

____

2. A *local context* is ____

____

Please check your definitions with the two in the Answer Key. Key.

■ ■ Cues within Local Contexts

Using local contexts to get help in identifying a word involves making predictions about it. Experience will tell you that making predictions about words is not unique to reading. In a conversation, for instance, anticipating what another is *about* to say is common, especially if the topic is familiar or if the speaker is hesitant or slow in speaking.

With both reading and listening, correct predictions about words are possible because (a) English is a positional language and (b) like all other languages, English makes sense. The first characteristic allows for *syntactic cues;* the second, for *semantic* cues. Each type will be discussed separately even though, in practice, readers use the two jointly.

Syntactic Cues

As was just mentioned, English is a *positional* language, which means that it relies heavily on word order to convey a message. Because it does, the position of a word in a sentence affects both the word's meaning and the meaning of the sentence. Changing word order, therefore, may alter meaning or destroy it altogether. The effect of word order is shown in the following arrangements of the same five words.

The man led the dog.

The dog led the man.

The led dog man the

The two arrangements that are sentences suggest a way to define *sentence:* a series of words that are ordered in a way that makes sense. Exactly how words are ordered in any given sentence constitutes its structure, or *syntax.* Using syntax to make inferences about words is thus referred to as using syntactic cues. Or, said somewhat differently, the help for word identifications that stems from word order is called a *syntactic cue.*

Use of syntactic cues does not lead directly to the identification of a word. Rather, it establishes limits on what it can be. Notice, for example, how the following order of words places constraints on what the omitted word can be.

That _____________ is very funny.

Limits established by the word order shown above reveal that the missing word is the name of something; that is, a noun. Since the omitted word bears a relationship to *is,* it is a singular noun. While information like "singular noun" is hardly enough to identify a word, combined with information deriving from other sources of help, it usually *is* sufficient.

TESTING

Before proceeding with the discussion of syntactic cues, let's stop to make sure that you are sufficiently familiar with two more terms that you can clearly explain them.

1. A *positional language* is ___________________________

____

2. A *syntactic cue* is ___________________________

____

Please see how your explanations correspond to those in the Answer Key.

Markers. As the discussion of syntax pointed up, syntactic cues allow for inferences about the kinds of words that fit at given points in a sentence. Certain kinds of words are especially informative about others and, for that reason, are called markers. A *marker* is a word that provides information about other words appearing in the same local context. Especially common are *noun markers.* These are words that indicate a noun will appear immediately (<u>that car</u>) or eventually (<u>that battered old car</u>). Notice all the noun markers in the following sentences.

An ___________ fell to the ___________.

Careless ___________ have been here.

Put their ___________ away.

That is Bill's ___________.

The can of ___________ is still open.

As the illustrative sentences indicate, noun markers are articles (<u>a</u>, <u>an</u>, <u>the</u>), adjectives (<u>careless</u>, <u>pretty</u>, <u>this</u>), possessive pronouns (<u>their</u>, <u>my</u>, <u>her</u>), possessive nouns (<u>Bill's</u>, <u>book's</u>, <u>door's</u>), and prepositions (<u>of</u>, <u>on</u>, <u>at</u>). Certain noun markers call for a singular noun (e.g., <u>an</u>, <u>this</u>); others, for a plural noun (e.g., <u>these</u>, <u>those</u>). Still other noun markers may be followed by a singular or a plural noun (e.g., <u>the</u>, <u>his</u>).

While noun markers are especially plentiful, other relationships among the words that constitute a sentence are also ready to assist readers; for they, too, suggest the grammatical function of a given word. To illustrate, let's assume in the sentences shown below that the omitted words are causing problems for a reader. On the basis of the other words, indicate what part of speech each unknown word is: pronoun, adjective, verb, adverb, article, preposition, or conjunction. The first sentence has been done to serve as an illustration.

1. I can't _____________ that fence.   (_____**verb**_____)

2. Don't put your feet _____________ anyone's chair.

   (_____________)

3. The room was _____________, small, and dark.

   (_____________)

4. The ice made the drink _____________.   (_____________)

5. I like cake, _____________ I like pie even better.

   (_____________)

6. The children _____________ up the fence.

   (_____________)

7. Try to walk _____________ so as not to bother him.

   (_____________)

8. _____________ bottle broke when it fell.   (_____________)

   Please compare your decisions with those in the Answer Key.

   The likelihood that you could respond to the above task quickly and correctly demonstrates not only your knowledge of English syntax but also the way in which syntactic cues allow readers to place restrictions on what an unknown word can be.

Semantic Cues

Still more constraints come from the meaning of the words that are known. For that reason, this second source of contextual help is referred to as a *semantic* cue. (Semantics, a branch of linguistics, is concerned with a study of meaning; hence, the name semantic cue.) Whereas syntactic cues inform a reader about the grammatical function of unknown words, semantic cues suggest which words with that particular function make sense. What makes sense, as the following contexts will demonstrate, depends on the meaning that is conveyed by the words that are known.

In each sentence below, syntax indicates that the missing word is a noun. The message conveyed by the other words suggests which noun is meaningful, thus likely to be the missing word. Using semantic cues, write in the blank the first noun that comes to mind as you read each sentence.

1. One ___________ on the car is flat.

2. Whenever I take an ___________, it never rains.

3. He has a ___________ and blue mark on his leg.

4. They have one ___________ and two sons.

5. The elevator isn't working, so you'll have to use the

___________.

Please check your responses with those listed in the Answer Key.

It seems safe to assume that what you found in the Answer Key matched your responses. Close or perfect agreement would be expected because all five sentences listed above are generous with semantic cues. Since you have just used them successfully, let's see whether you can now define *semantic cue.*

A *semantic cue* is ________________________

____

Even though there is no one best way to verbalize the meaning of semantic cue, compare your definition with the one in the Answer Key to make sure that yours includes the essential points.

As was just demonstrated, semantic cues can be rich sources of help for word identifications; however, they cannot always be counted on to eliminate practically everything except one word as did those you just worked with. Semantic cues are present in the following sentences, yet they do not provide as much constraint as the earlier examples.

How many _______________ are in the book? (pages, pictures, words, . . .)

Her dress was blue, _______________, and white. (black, green, yellow, . . .)

They like to play in the _______________. (street, basement, park, . . .)

And some sentences provide no semantic help. For example:

That is very _______________.

Have you ever _______________?

_______________ is here.

Even though a local context may provide little or no semantic help, some might be available in the general context—that is, in the story, article, or paragraph in which the unknown or forgotten word occurs. Help may even be as close as the preceding or following sentence:

I get up late. That's why I don't eat any _______________.

Now he's out of _______________. He jogged too much.

As the preceding examples show, semantic cues are not restricted—as are syntactic cues—to the sentence containing the word causing problems.

Teachers need to keep one other point in mind whenever they consider work with contexts as a way of facilitating word identifications. It can be made with the help of two closely similar sentences:

The American flag is red, white, and _______________.

The French flag is red, white, and _______________.

Each sentence above offers identical kinds and amounts of contextual help. In both, syntactic cues joined with semantic cues (plus punctuation) clearly indicate that the two missing words name colors. In spite of the identical assistance, however, it is safe to predict—at least for American readers—that the omitted word in the second sentence may remain unknown even though the color word in the first sentence will be supplied spontaneously. Obviously, background knowledge accounts for the difference. Teachers who remember the critical importance of background knowledge for reading are always looking for ways to add to children's experiences, understandings, and concepts, as well as the vocabulary that goes with all three; for when all three are limited, corresponding limitations are placed on a child's potential for success with reading.

TESTING

What to cover when instructing children about contextual cues will be considered next. First, though, let's see whether you can respond successfully to another request.

Assume that the boxed material that follows is an outline. Write a paragraph that explains how each heading and subheading relates to the title, "Predictions about Unknown Words." Once you've done that, compare your paragraph with the one in the Answer Key.

Predictions about Unknown Words

Background Knowledge
Oral Vocabulary
General Context
Local Context
    Syntactic Cue
    Semantic Cue

____

____

____

■ ■ Helping Children Use Contextual Cues

Helping students use contexts to get help with a word is important because it is one step toward independent children who can solve their own reading problems. And it will be highly productive of correct identifications, assuming not too many words are causing problems. That condition must be mentioned because too many unknowns lead to an excessively slow rate of reading that, in turn, obstructs the child's sense both of syntax and of meaning. Who, after all, can hang on to the sense of a sentence like the following?

The ________________ ________________ so quickly that ________ ________ couldn't ________________.

What the above clearly shows is that a context comes close to going out of existence when large numbers of words are unknown. Therefore, in addition to helping children use contexts, teachers must give ample time to the development of sizable vocabularies to ensure that most words *will* be known. When they are, contextual cues will help the reader identify the unknown ones.[1]

As it happens, attention to contextual cues can be initiated before children are able to do any reading. This is so because, like written text, spoken language has contexts.

Using Spoken Language

When children first enter school, they already understand a great deal about language. Although they cannot explain or

____

[1] A child's *sight vocabulary* consists of all the words that he or she is able to identify instantaneously; that is, "on sight." How teachers can foster extensive sight vocabularies with the help of interesting practice has been treated elsewhere (4, 5).

categorize even a little of what they know, they habitually demonstrate their functional, intuitive knowledge both when they speak and when they comprehend what others say. Because young children do know so much about language, the use of contexts to make predictions about words is possible before any reading ability exists.

A kindergarten teacher who appreciates both the language sophistication of her students and the value of contexts for word identification might say something like the following to five-year-olds, none of whom can read.

I thought you might like to play detective today. In this game, you're on the lookout for a word. You'll know what the word is if you listen to the clues I give. I'll say something, but I won't finish it. Your job as detectives is to listen to what I say, then tell me the word that I didn't say. Let's do one together so that you'll know how the game works. Listen. What's the word that I don't say? "In our room, we have eleven boys and thirteen ____________." . . . Correct! I knew you'd be good detectives because you're good listeners. Let's do another one. This time, if you know the word I don't say, raise your hand. "Yesterday it was raining at 10:30, so we couldn't go outside to ____________." . . . Right. I thought you'd remember that you weren't able to play outside yesterday.

At another time, mind reading can provide more opportunities for children to generate words for specified contexts.

Sometimes, mothers and daddies know so much about us that it seems they know what we're thinking even before we say it. They can almost read our minds, can't they? Let's see whether you can read my mind. I'll say something, but I'll leave out one word. I'll think of the word, but won't say it. When I come to the word I'm thinking but not saying, I'll raise my hand. Listen. "On Friday, the high school ____________ is coming to play for us." . . . "We need to get plenty of sleep at night so that we won't be ____________ in school." . . .

Pictured objects can also figure in oral practice. Now, children will select displayed pictures in order to complete such spoken sentences as the following:

I like to look out the ____________. (picture of a window)

In summer, we swim in a ____________. (picture of a pool)

The boy on the _______________ is going too fast.   (picture of
a bicycle)

Those _______________ are from our garden.   (picture of
flowers)

The illustrations of how children's facility with spoken language allows for early practice in using contexts suggest two
guidelines for instruction:

1. At the start, omitted words should be at, or close to, the end
   of the sentence so that a maximum of contextual help will
   be available. Gradually, their position in a sentence should
   be varied.

2. Any response from the children is acceptable as long as it is
   both syntactically and semantically consistent with the other
   words in the context. The emphasis (as in reading) is on the
   fact that language makes sense.

Using Spoken Language
and Minimal Graphophonic Cues

Commonly, children begin to learn letter names and some
letter sounds in kindergarten, so spoken language for context
practice can soon be superseded by spoken language plus
minimal graphophonic cues. Since the sounds that initial vowel
letters record vary in relation to other letters is the same syllable (e.g., am, aim), the first type of graphophonic cue used is
initial consonants. A teacher might get started by asking:

*What's the name of this letter [pointing to a card displaying t]?
...Who can tell us a word that starts with the sound that this
letter stands for? . . . Good. Two, toe, and Tom all start with
the sound that goes with this letter. Now I'm going to think of
a word that starts with t, but I won't tell you what it is. I want
to see if you can guess the word I'm thinking of. Here goes.
We have two pets in our room. One is a _______________. Right.
One is a turtle. How did you know I wasn't thinking of our
gerbil? . . . Right, gerbil doesn't begin with the right sound.
It doesn't begin with the sound that this letter [pointing to t]
makes. Let's try another one. . . .*

On another day, the sound getting attention is the one associated with p. Now the teacher says:

I'm thinking of a word that starts with the sound that goes with this letter [points to p]. See if you can read my mind. My favorite color is ________________. [One child suggests purple and another pink.] Why couldn't the answer be pencil? Pencil starts with p. [And now all the children explain, "That isn't a color!"]

Even though minimal visual help (one letter) is being offered to these beginners, the activity does show how teachers can take one step toward written text, which offers not only contextual cues for word identifications but also maximum graphophonic cues. Until children are able to use total spellings, practice like that just described should be provided regularly in conjunction with phonics instruction.

Using Written Contexts at the Beginning

Since reading is a response to print, not to spoken language, written contexts should enter into practice as soon as possible. Once reading vocabularies begin to develop, written sentences like the following are appropriate for other kinds of work with contexts.

We have a ball and a ________________.
play   bat

I want to ________________ the horse.
see   look

________________ you come?
Car   Can

If the children who work with sentences like those shown above are able to print, they should be asked to fill in each blank with the correct word. This is preferable to having them underline it, since writing a word fosters attention to the sequence of its letters. That attention is important because the only feature that distinguishes some words from others is the sequence of their letters (e.g., no, on; left, felt; saw, was).

Using Written Contexts and Minimal Graphophonic Cues

When children are able to read some words and also know some letter-sound relationships, another kind of practice can be initiated. Then, a teacher might say to a group of children:

As you can see, all the sentences on the sheet I just gave you have a missing word. Its first letter is there, though, so if you'll think of the sound that goes with that letter, you'll know what the missing word is. Look at the first sentence. To yourself, read all the words that are there; then think what the missing word might be. Remember, it begins with the letter s. . . . Who thinks they know what the missing word is? . . . That's right. When you put in the missing word, the sentence says, "It is hot in the sun." Let me show you what sun looks like so that you can see that it starts with an s. . . . Why did you think of sun and not afternoon? After all, it gets very hot in the afternoon. . . .

Another way to provide practice in the combined use of written contexts and limited graphophonic cues is described below. It, too, can be used when reading vocabularies and knowledge of letter-sound relationships are meager. This particular activity demonstrates what often occurs in reading; namely, contextual cues suggest sensible possibilities, and graphophonic cues help determine which possibility is correct.

I've written a sentence on the board, but it has one word missing. [I can open the _______________ with my key.] Who think they know what the missing word might be? . . . Okay. Tom thinks it's door. Does anyone think it might be another word? . . . Let's see now. There have been five suggestions that make sense—door, box, safe, suitcase, and drawer. The letter the missing word begins with is written on the back of this little card. What letter is this? . . . Since it's b, what word should I write to finish the sentence? . . . Why? . . .

Using Written Contexts and Additional Graphophonic Cues

The more letter-sound relationships children know, the more ready they are to use the constraints that come from total spellings to identify an unknown word. Written practice that uses more than just initial letters can dwell on sentences like the following:

Our football t_________m won.

St___________m can burn you.

We'll fish in the str____________m.

While children are still in the process of learning how to cope with the variability of vowel sounds, they should be helped to see that fairly short words can often be figured out by using consonant letters only—if contexts are considered, too. How word fragments can enter into word-identification practice is illustrated next.

Children should w___rk in school.

Don't d___v___ into that water.

The dog's h___nd foot has a cut.

Can you pl______ this game?

Once children have learned about the need to divide an unknown word into syllables before attempting to figure it out, they are ready to learn that knowing the pronunciation of the first syllable in a word may be enough to suggest what the whole of it says—if contextual cues are used, too. For example:

He is the pi__________ of the plane.

I need some but__________ for my bread.

Boil the water in this ket__________.

In addition to showing the value of contextual help and, secondly, how the whole of a word doesn't always have to be worked on to achieve its identification, the three sentences above also demonstrate—once again—the important role played by experiences (and the vocabulary that goes with them). Clearly, children who know that pilots fly planes, that butter goes on bread, and that water is sometimes boiled in a kettle are the ones who would be most successful in figuring out the incomplete words shown above.

Success is also fostered by teachers who help their students see the connection between school exercises and real reading. Such teachers never forget to remind children to use contexts and as many letters as necessary whenever they come across a word they don't know.

A progression for school exercises is summarized in Table 2.1.

■ ■ Other Work with Contexts

Contexts are also helpful—sometimes even mandatory—for working out problems concerned with meaning. How contexts

---

■ ■ TABLE 2.1 Progression for Practice in Using Contextual Cues

---

1. *Spoken Context*
   (a) Word omitted at end of sentence
   (b) Word omitted elsewhere

2. *Spoken Context* plus Minimal Graphophonic Cues
   Initial letter of omitted word supplied

3. *Written Context*
   Word omitted

4. *Written Context* plus Minimal Graphophonic Cues
   Initial letter of omitted word supplied

5. *Written Context* plus Additional Graphophonic Cues
   (a) Initial and final letter of omitted word supplied
   (b) All consonant letters of omitted word supplied
   (c) Spelling of initial syllable in omitted word supplied

6. *Written Context* plus Total Graphophonic Cues
   Unknown word placed in sentence

---

enter into word meanings is especially apparent with *homonyms:* words having identical spellings but different meanings The significance of contexts for such words is illustrated below.

The dog will soon be here.

The dog days of summer will soon be here.

Sometimes, both the pronunciation and the meaning of identically spelled words vary, depending on the way they function in a given context. For example:

You are close to the door.

Please close it.

She has a tear in her dress.

She also has a tear in her eye.

As children become more advanced in their reading ability, they need to learn about shifts in stress (rébel, rebél), which result not only in altered pronunciations but also in different meanings. Again, contexts must be featured:

His conduct is excellent.

He should conduct the meeting.

That is a beautiful object.

I object to painting it.

Even though the pronunciation of most words remains constant, the meaning they convey can vary considerably—again, depending on the context in which they are embedded. This is demonstrated below with the "simple" word <u>cross</u>.

Cross the street carefully.

Don't cross that bridge until you come to it.

A cross is on the top of the church.

He was so cross when I was late.

That seems to be my cross in life.

This street will soon cross with that road.

He's a cross between a terrier and a spaniel.

Please cross out all wrong answers.

In addition to displaying the significance of contexts for word meanings, sentences like those listed above underscore the *lack* of significance in such classroom practices as having children use dictionaries to look up the meanings of isolated words arranged in a column. Why each word should be placed in one or more contexts should now be clear.

Being demonstrated by *all* the illustrations in this chapter is that various uses of contexts are of great importance for reading and, in addition, that attention to them can begin early and ought to continue throughout elementary school.

TESTING

Summarizing what one has tried to teach is a good practice for instructors to follow at all grade levels. Since it is, the self-testing that is appropriate now is one that pulls together some of the main points made in the chapter about the use of contextual cues.

Please fill in the blanks below.

English is a _______________ language in which word order is highly important for determining _______________. The word order that makes up any sentence is referred to as its _______________; consequently, when the position of an unknown word in a sentence helps to identify it, that help is known as a _______________ cue. Syntactic cues provide assistance by establishing the part of speech of any word in a sentence. With nouns, they also indicate number; with verbs, tense. In a sentence such as "Various _______________ were there," syntax indicates the omitted word is a _______________ _______________.

Just as language as a whole makes sense, so too must individual sentences. The sense, or meaning, conveyed by sentences provides still another type of contextual cue. Since it has to do with meaning, it is called a _______________ cue. A sentence like "Various _______________ were there" exemplifies minimal semantic help. On the other hand, one like "Pass the _______________ and pepper" exemplifies _______________ semantic help.

Because the _______________ use of syntactic and semantic cues often provides a reader with a great deal of assistance in identifying an _______________ word, children should be encouraged to look to them immediately whenever they have trouble with a word. Sometimes—as in "Pass the _______________ and pepper"—contextual cues will offer such generous and obvious help that all words except one can be _______________ from consideration. In most cases, however, contextual cues will have to be used in conjunction with the help that derives from the _______________ of the unfamiliar word.

Please check your responses with those in the Answer Key.

■ ■ A Concluding Comment

One final comment now seems in order. It has to do with a question that might have arisen as you read the chapter: In instructing children about contexts, should I use terms like *noun, semantic,* and *syntax?* To respond, let me make a distinction between younger and older children for a reason that will soon be clear.

For younger children, such terms are totally foreign. What is very familiar, on the other hand, is use of contexts, because children and adults alike rely on them routinely whenever they are attending to spoken language. Encouraging children to use written contexts to help with words, therefore, is getting them to do what comes naturally. Consequently, the need for terms like noun and syntax is nonexistent.

As children progress to second and third grades, language lessons begin to teach the meanings of terms related to grammar. Only when children thoroughly understand them should such terms enter into instruction. Now they will be able to facilitate communication between teacher and student (e.g., "Is the word you don't know going to be a singular or a plural noun?"). A more general guideline for teaching might be stated as follows: Instruction should include only what will help achieve its goal. Since attention to contexts has as its goal the correct identification of unfamiliar words, it follows that only what will assist with that objective should enter into instruction.

USE OF PHONICS TO IDENTIFY WORDS

Oral Language and Phonics

Knowledge Required to Derive
  Pronunciations from Spellings

What Decoders Need to Be Able to Do

As was mentioned in Chapter 2, English has an alphabetic writing system. This means that words are recorded, or spelled, on the basis of their pronunciation. More specifically, it means that connections exist between letters and speech sounds. What readers need to know and be able to do in order to move from letters to pronunciations is the subject of this chapter. The ability to make such moves is important because if a word that is unfamiliar visually is familiar to the reader in its spoken form, the pronunciation will signal meaning:

$$\boxed{\text{book}} \longrightarrow \text{pronunciation} \longrightarrow \text{meaning}$$

■ ■ Oral Language and Phonics

What should not be forgotten about the above progression is the role oral language plays. How that enters into a reader's efforts to identify puzzling words has been underscored explicitly and clearly by Roger Brown, a linguist. He notes:

The usefulness of being able to sound a new word depends on the state of the reader's speaking vocabulary. If the word that is unfamiliar in printed form is also unfamiliar in spoken form the reader who can sound it out will not understand the word any better than the reader who cannot sound it. . . . the real advantage in being able to sound a word that is unfamiliar in print, only appears when the word is familiar in speech. The child's letter-by-letter pronunciation, put together by spelling recipe, will, with the aid of context, call to mind the spoken form. There will be a click of recognition, pronunciation will smooth out, and meaning will transfer to the printed form. The ability to sound out new words is not simply a pronunciation skill; it is a technique for expanding reading comprehension vocabulary to the size of speaking comprehension vocabulary. This is a considerable help since speaking vocabulary is likely to be ten times the size of reading vocabulary for the primary child. [1, p. 69]

Not to be overlooked in Brown's observations is that oral vocabularies facilitate shifts from approximately correct to precisely correct pronunciations. Such adjustments are often necessary with words of more than syllable. With one like <u>condone</u>, for instance, connections between letters and sounds (graphophonic cues) suggest the pronunciation "cŏn-dōnø." Readers who are familiar with <u>condone</u> in its spoken form will be able to shift to the correct pronunciation if they are wise enough to use graphophonic cues *in conjunction with* contextual cues:

I cannot condone their lies.

It should be noted that for readers who are not familiar with *condone* in its written *or* its spoken form, a pronunciation such as "cŏn-dōnø" will seem just as acceptable as "cŭn-dōnø"; and this will be the case even if they use contextual cues.

What this statement underscores, then, is that even though this chapter singles out graphophonic cues for special consideration, the contributions of oral vocabularies to word identifications should be neither forgotten nor underestimated.

TESTING

Before we move on, let's stop to pull together what has been said thus far. First, let's see if you can define oral vocabulary.

A child's *oral vocabulary* is _______________________________________

____

Please check your definition with the one in the Answer Key. Then respond to the following request.

Currently, some kindergartens are spending so much time on phonics that too little is left for developing oral vocabularies. In a paragraph, explain why attention to the latter would contribute substantially to the children's eventual success with phonics. When your paragraph is finished, check its content with the sample paragraph in the Answer Key.

____

____

____

■ ■ ■ Knowledge Required to Derive Pronunciations from Spellings

Because it is unrealistic to expect all unknown words to be in contexts that are overflowing with syntactic and semantic prompts, children need to be prepared to make maximum use of spellings to achieve correct identifications. As was mentioned in Chapter 1, knowledgeable use of spellings is helpful in two ways: It reveals information about a word's structure and about its pronunciation. Using spellings to learn about structure is the theme of Chapter 4. What children (a) need to know and (b) need to be able to do in order to use spellings to arrive at pronunciations is the concern now.

What children need to know if spellings are to yield correct pronunciations can be divided into general knowledge and specific knowledge, the latter being concerned with terminology, syllabication, letter-sound relationships, factors that affect letter-sound relationships, and stressed syllables. Let's deal with general knowledge first, then we'll go on to each type of specific knowledge.

General Knowledge

What children need to know as soon as possible is that what is taught about spellings and pronunciations has nothing to do with rules—if by "rule" is meant "something that always works." That kind of reliability is unavailable because the correspondence between letters and sounds in English is not perfectly consistent. Pairs of words like <u>have</u> and <u>cave</u>, <u>toe</u> and <u>shoe</u>, and <u>colonel</u> and <u>colonial</u> demonstrate this.

Fortunately, enough consistency does exist to allow for generalizations; that is, for statements of what is generally characteristic of the way English words are recorded. Such statements are taught in phonics because if they are used with flexibility and in conjunction with contextual cues, they can be highly productive for achieving correct pronunciations.

Let me be more specific with the help of two generalizations:

The letter g stands for two sounds. One is called its *soft* sound (gem, gym); the other, its *hard* sound (go, gum).

Generally, g stands for the soft sound when it is followed by e, i, or y (ginger). Otherwise it is likely to record the hard sound (glad).

Children taught by knowledgeable, competent teachers will understand from the above generalizations that *most of the time,* g followed by e will record the soft sound. Consequently, should they come across gear in The gear shift won't move, and they don't know what it says, they would try the soft sound for g. In fact, they might simply add that sound to a word they know —ear. Realizing that the additional sound fails to produce anything that is meaningful in the given context, they would next try the hard sound, which does yield a sensible word.

Children like those just described are displaying what is essential if generalizations are to be productive: flexible use. Teachers who want to promote flexibility make sure that children understand the basic nature of phonic generalizations. And they also make sure that practice in applying them is carried on with unknown words placed in contexts, since what is sensible depends on the sentence in which the word causing problems is embedded.

Teachers who want to heighten the value of phonics instruction also make certain that children know that generalizations are applied to syllables, not to words. With single syllable words, of course, no such distinction is necessary. However, with multisyllable words—the kind that causes most problems—the distinction is essential. Again, let me illustrate this point with an example.

Children who have learned that aw stands for a single sound (e.g., law), but who forget to consider the syllabication of an unknown word prior to considering sounds for letters, will have problems with words like away and aware. On the other hand, children who consider syllabication first (with guidelines coming from generalizations that will soon be referred to) would know when aw must be considered as a unit (aw ful) and when a and w function separately (a ware).

Two points about contexts that are also relevant to this discussion were made in Chapter 2. First, a helpful context often means that an unfamiliar word's spelling may only have to be used to confirm (or question) the correctness of what the context indicates the word is. Second, with a helpful context, only part of an unknown word may have to be figured out in order to identify the whole of it. You will recall that the two points were illustrated with contexts like these:

a. One *tire* on the car is flat.

b. He is the *pilot* of the plane.

The two points are important because the faster unfamiliar words are figured out, the less likely it is that they will impede comprehension.

A Summary

The general knowledge that children eventually need to acquire if graphophonic cues are to be maximally helpful can now be summarized as follows.

1. The application of phonic generalizations to words that are visually unfamiliar provides a starting point that might or might not result in a correct identification. Applying them, therefore, should be viewed as a type of problem solving in which the first "answer" is not necessarily right.

2. Since phonic generalizations are not rules that always work, they must be used in conjunction with the syntactic and semantic help that derives from contexts.

3. Generalizations are applied to syllables, not to words. Therefore, the syllabication of an unfamiliar word should be dealt with before generalizations about letter-sound relationships are considered.

4. The amount of attention given the spelling of an unknown word will be affected by the amount of contextual help that is available. When that help is generous, a spelling may have to be used only as a quick check on what the context indicates the word is. At other times, contextual help may mean that only part of the unknown word has to be worked

on. At still other times, the whole of a word may have to be carefully analyzed because contextual help is so meager.

Terminology

The specific knowledge children need in order to use graphophonic cues for word identifications is fairly substantial. Fortunately, it does not have to be acquired immediately. Instead, what needs to be known can accumulate gradually with the help of carefully planned practice. Since some of the specific knowledge relates to terminology, let's deal with that initially.

Using spellings to figure out pronunciations is called *decoding.* Since decoding moves from letters to speech sounds, some of the terms concerned with this process pertain to letters and others refer to sounds. The terminology concerned with letters will be considered first. (Be sure to take enough time to memorize definitions, since the terms will appear frequently throughout the chapter.)

Letters. Technically, *vowel* and *consonant* refer to sounds; however, in phonics they are used to refer to letters. The letters that are called vowels are a, e, i, o, and u. The other twenty-one letters are consonants. (Y and w are consonants, but—as subsequent pages will show—they sometimes function as if they were vowels.)

Grapheme (gră-phēmę) is a term that reflects the linguistic influence on phonics. Linguists use *grapheme* to refer to the symbols (letters) that represent speech sounds. Although *grapheme* is not a term that would be used with children, teachers should be familiar with it, since it is found in some instructional materials.

The related term *graphemic base* is also found in materials. It is a synonym for *phonogram.* The two terms refer to certain sequences of letters made up of a vowel followed by one or more consonants (e.g., -ung, -ight, -ank, -it). Since such sequences often compose parts of syllables (e.g., sung, night, tank, hit), they receive attention in phonics instruction.

Digraph, as its spelling suggests, refers to two letters. In phonics, it refers to a pair of letters that stands for one sound. Digraphs include both consonants (sh, ch, th, ph, gh, ng) and vowels (oo, au, ou, oi). That a digraph records one sound is illustrated in words like shop and ooze.

Other pairs of letters (e.g., bl, st, cr) stand for two sounds (e.g., blame, star, crop). Because these pairs—always consonants—appear frequently in syllables, they also receive attention in phonics, since the ability to deal with more than one letter at a time speeds up the decoding process. Consonants that often appear as successive letters are called *clusters,* which helps to set them apart from the digraphs referred to above.[1]

Table 3.1 should assist you in making a distinction between clusters and digraphs. In particular, it should point up that the number of sounds that a cluster represents is equal to the number of letters that compose it. In contrast, each digraph stands for one sound.

Sounds.   Speech sounds, referred to by linguists as *phonemes* (phō-nēmͤ), divide into vowels and consonants on the basis of physiological and acoustical characteristics.[2] Fifteen *vowel*

■ ■ **TABLE 3.1 Clusters and Digraphs**

Consonant Clusters

bl	fl	sc	st
br	fr	sk	sw
cl	gl	sl	tr
cr	gr	sm	tw
dr	pl	sn	scr
dw	pr	sp	str

Consonant Digraphs

ph (phone)   ch (chap, chef)

gh (rough)   th (the, thin)

sh (shell)   ng (rang)

Vowel Digraphs

oo (cool, cook)

au, aw (auto, awe)

ou, ow (out, owl)

oi, oy (oil, oyster)

---

[1] Rarely, a cluster will be three successive consonants (*scr, str*). In these cases, the cluster stands for a blend of three sounds.

[2] Since this chapter is concerned with phonics, not with the highly detailed and technical study of speech sounds known as phonetics, subtleties that are so important for that technical study will not be considered or even mentioned. Technically, for instance, the division of speech sounds is far more complicated than has been suggested. For phonics, however, the more general classifications *vowel* and *consonant* are sufficient. Any reader interested in technical details of speech sounds might want to examine *Phonics, Linguistics, and Reading* (3).

sounds are considered in phonics instruction. They are represented by the underlined letters in the words that follow.

am	ate	took
elf	eel	tool
is	ice	caught
odd	old	oil
us	use	out

As can be seen in the third column, five vowel sounds are recorded with digraphs. Be sure you can hear all fifteen sounds before proceeding. (Say each word aloud, then pronounce its vowel sound.)

The *consonant sounds* that get attention in phonics are represented by the underlined letters in the following words.

but	job	pull	we
do	key	ran	yet
for	let	sit	zoo
gum	my	to	
he	no	van	

The term *blend* needs to be mentioned in this discussion, for it is used to refer to the synthesis, or combination, of sounds that clusters stand for. The clusters that are underlined in the words below each represent a blend of two sounds. (Read the words aloud to make sure that you hear the two sounds that go with each cluster.)

dry	gray	small	sweet
flee	slow	spell	twig

Contrasts like the following should help you hear that a digraph records one sound, whereas a cluster stands for a blend of sounds.

shop	phone	thin
crop	drone	spin

As was mentioned earlier, linguists refer to speech sounds as *phonemes.* In order to distinguish between graphemes and phonemes, they use slash marks (/   /) to refer to the latter. Thus, b refers to a letter, while /b/ refers to the sound that b stands for. It could be said, then, that b stands for /b/, that f stands for /f/, and so on.

One other term should be mentioned even though it is not necessary to use it with children. I refer to *diphthong* (dif́-thong). What oi represents in oil and what ou stands for in out are diphthongs.

Technically, a diphthong is a close blend of two vowel sounds; however, since diphthongs are commonly perceived as being one sound, phonics instruction treats the digraphs oi, oy, ou, and ow as if each stood for one vowel sound in words like coin, oyster, our, and owl.

TESTING

Presumably, some of the terms that have been discussed were familiar to you before you read the chapter. Now is a good time to review any that were new. Then proceed with the testing.

As the discussion of terms pointed out, some pertain to letters and others pertain to sounds. With that in mind, divide the following terms into two columns, one called "Letters" and the other "Sounds": *blend, cluster, digraph, diphthong, grapheme, graphemic base, phoneme, phonogram.*

Please check your division with the Answer Key.

Five terms that might have been new will appear in subsequent pages. To make sure you understand them, please define the following.

1. *Decoding* is _______________________________________

____

2. A *cluster* is _______________________________________

____

3. A *blend* is _______________________________

____

4. A *digraph* is _______________________________

____

5. A *phonogram* is _______________________________

____

Please check your five definitions with those in the Answer Key.

To relate this discussion of phonic terms to classroom practices, another type of testing is called for. This time, let's see how well you can critique the three statements shown below, all of which were heard in classrooms. All are incorrect for reasons that should now be clear. Following each statement, therefore, explain *why* it is incorrect.

1. "In the following words, circle all the blends."

____

____

2. "A digraph is one sound spelled with two letters."

____

____

3. "What sound do you see at the end of plant?"

____

____

Please check your explanations with those in the Answer Key.

Syllabication

In order to move from spellings to pronunciations, children need to know about syllabication, since it is syllables that are decoded, not words.

Even though it *is* syllables that are decoded, a distinction does not have to be made between *syllable* and *word* when phonics instruction begins. While teaching about the connection between f and /f/, for instance, teachers might use words like <u>fun</u>, <u>fast</u>, and <u>fix</u> for illustrative purposes and never refer to syllables. Even if words like <u>family</u> and <u>fever</u> are among the illustrations, a reference still does not have to be made to syllables—in fact, none should be made until children learn about vowel sounds. This is so because a syllable *is* a vowel sound, to which consonant sounds are typically added.

Once children know some vowel sounds and, in addition, begin to encounter multisyllabic words with some frequency in whatever it is they are reading, the need exists to teach them (a) what a syllable is and (b) how to divide unknown words into syllables so that each syllable can be decoded.

What a Syllable Is. As was just mentioned, a *syllable* is a vowel sound to which consonant sounds are usually added. Various kinds of syllables are shown below:

able	solo	partner	author	maintain	picture
a ble	so lo	part ner	au thor	main tain	pic ture

To emphasize that the focus is vowel sounds, not vowel letters, the following words should help; for, although some of them contain more than one vowel letter, each is one syllable because each has but one vowel sound:

so	heel	change	strength	clause	squeeze

The individual sounds that compose a syllable may appear in initial, medial, or final positions. With a syllable like <u>hit</u>, h stands for the initial sound, <u>i</u> for the medial sound, and t for the final sound. In the case of a more complex syllable such as <u>stoop</u>, <u>st</u> stands for the initial sounds, <u>oo</u> for the medial sound, and <u>p</u> for the final sound. A syllable like <u>ac</u> has only initial and final sounds.

Even though syllabication does not enter into beginning phonics instruction, it will be the first topic discussed under "What Children Need to Know" because all the phonic generalizations that are presented in subsequent pages focus on syllables, not on words.

Dividing Words into Syllables.   If you are able to read a word, you can *hear* its syllables. Because you can read <u>picnic</u>, for instance, you can hear the two syllables "pic" and "nic." As you read each word listed below, divide it into its syllables in the way I have divided <u>picnic</u>.

picnic	signal	tablet
pic nic		
chimney	monsoon	success

Please check your divisions with those in the Answer Key.

To be remembered is that children who cannot read the words you just syllabicated do not hear anything when they encounter them in print. <u>Signal</u>, for example, would be a string of six letters and nothing more. Yet, if children can't read <u>signal</u>, they have to divide it into syllables to decode it, since all the generalizations about letter-sound relationships are based on syllables. How can this be accomplished?

The only way to make a decision about the syllabication of <u>signal</u> (or any other unknown word) is to use its spelling, that is, its letters and their sequence. To see how this works, consider the words you just divided into syllables. Is there a pattern in their spellings that suggests a syllabic division—one that could be used by children who cannot read them? When you've arrived at a generalization about the pattern, write it below. Then check the correctness of your observation with the generalization in the Answer Key.

____

____

If you arrived at a generalization that was unknown to you prior to the exercise, you arrived at it *inductively*. You began with specifics (in this case, six words), and you moved to a statement that described visual cues (letters and their sequence) that suggest a syllabic division. More specifically, your statement pointed up that all six words have the pattern VCCV (vowel, consonant, consonant, vowel) and, in addition, that all divide into syllables between the two consonants—for instance, sig nal.

Inductive phonics instruction is often recommended for children with the hope that it will foster a better understanding of generalizations and, further, that it will enable them to make systematic observations about written words. It is viewed, then, as a way of helping them learn how to learn on their own.

While nobody could dispute the importance of such an objective, an exclusive use of inductive teaching slows down phonics instruction to such an extent that children learn many generalizations long after they would have found them useful for their reading. Exclusive reliance on inductive procedures could also create a teacher who loses sight of the reason for phonics, which is a very practical one: to enable children to figure out the identity of unknown words. With that as the goal, phonics programs must always be evaluated not in relation to how well they promote inductive reasoning, but in relation to how successful children are in decoding. When the correct goal is kept in mind, some combination of inductive and deductive teaching will be elected.[3]

Deductive teaching, unlike inductive, proceeds by telling. In Table 3.2, I tell you very directly about other generalizations

---

■ ■ **TABLE 3.2 Syllabicating Unknown Words Using Visual Cues**

When two consonants that are not digraphs are between two vowels, the word generally divides into syllables between the consonants. For instance:

signal (sig nal)   matter (mat ter)   adventure (ad ven ture)

When one consonant is between two vowels, a syllabic division usually occurs before the consonant.* For instance: instance:

open (o pen)   thesis (the sis)   arena (a re na)

When a word ends in a consonant followed by *le,* the consonant plus *le* are a syllable. For instance:

able (a ble)   kindle (kin dle)   article (ar ti cle)

* An exception occurs when the consonant is x, as in axis and exit. Then, the first vowel and x are in the same syllable (ax is, ex it).

---

[3] How to teach generalizations to children both inductively and deductively is described and illustrated elsewhere (4, 5).

that pinpoint visual cues for syllabicating unknown or forgotten words. They are listed along with the generalization already referred to. Study each one, *making sure you see how the examples illustrate the generalization.* Following the telling, there will be some testing.

TESTING

To see whether you can apply the generalizations, divide the following nonsense words into groups so that each group has the same syllabication pattern.

baple	gixas	nefut	sticess
durcle	honat	phanitt	thoftan
ento	idfer	rinfle	uxot

Next, state the generalization that describes each pattern. (Teachers must be able to verbalize a pattern when they are explaining it to children. That is why you are asked to state the generalizations.) Once you have, compare your groups of nonsense words and statements with those in the Answer Key.

When you checked the statements of generalizations in the Answer Key, you probably noticed that the wording of some was different from what was used when the generalizations were stated originally. The changes were deliberate and were made in order to show that a generalization can be verbalized in more than one way. Nonetheless, every statement must contain essential details. With that in mind, describe the omission in the following statement that makes it unacceptable.

If the first vowel in a word is followed by two consonants, the first syllable usually ends with the first of the two consonants.

Omission: ____

Please check your explanation with the one in the Answer Key. Why is the following statement also incorrect?

In all of the following words, /b/ is a medial sound: number, gable, album, and symbol.

Error: ________________________________

____

Again, compare your explanation with the one in the Answer Key.

You should now be ready to pinpoint a basic flaw in the generalization stated below. (It was found in a workbook.) Following the statement, explain why it is a useless generalization for decoders.

"If the first vowel in a word has a long sound and is followed by a single consonant, the first syllable usually ends with the vowel, as in spi der, la dy, and o cean."

____

____

____

The correct explanation is in the Answer Key.

Additional Points about Syllabication. As children begin to encounter longer and longer words, they have to deal with more and more syllables. Consequently, the need to use more than one generalization with a word becomes common. For the syllabication of article, for instance, two different generalizations are required. (Which two?) For words like consonant and lumbago, two generalizations also are needed. (Which two?) With chimpanzee and embargo, on the other hand, one generalization has to be applied twice. (Which one?) To divide aroma, a child would have to apply another generalization twice. (Which one?) In the case of kindergarten, the same generalization would be applied three times. (Which one?)

As words become more difficult, it is also important for children to remember that the special digraphs (e.g., ph and au) function as if they were but one letter when unknown words are divided into syllables. This is illustrated by the examples in Table 3.3, in which words are grouped according to two of the spelling patterns that have significance for syllabication.

■ ■ ■ **TABLE 3.3 How Two Spelling Patterns Affect Syllabication**

VCCV = VC CV			VCV = V CV		
organ	or	gan	acorn	a	corn
orphan	or	phan	aphid	a	phid
aster	as	ter	saber	sa	ber
austere	aus	tere	saucer	sau	cer

Knowing about clusters (consonants that often appear together in syllables) helps decoders syllabicate unknown words in which three successive consonants occur. For instance:

pilgrim	parsnip	constant	monster
pil grim	par snip	con stant	mon ster

Once readers divide an unknown word into syllables with the assistance of visual cues (letters and their sequence), they are ready to work out the sounds of each syllable so that they can be combined to yield the word's pronunciation. If the word is in their oral vocabulary, the pronunciation will yield meaning.

A Perspective for Decoding

Before dealing with what children need to know about letters and sounds in order to achieve pronunciations, let's consider the possible strategies of one decoder as he works on the unfamiliar word <u>plastic</u>, embedded in the sentence <u>They make belts out of plastic.</u> Even though other successful decoders might use different strategies, his will provide some perspective for the ensuing discussion of additional content for phonics instruction.

His thoughts proceed as follows:

Well, it isn't "leather" because that begins with <u>l</u>. My mother has a straw belt, but it isn't "straw" either. I'll divide it between <u>s</u> and <u>t</u>. There couldn't be more than two syllables because there are only two vowels. Let's see—p, l, a, s. One vowel and it's not at the end of the syllable. That probably means the short sound for <u>a</u>. That would be ă, plă, plăs. Plăs?

I can't think of any word that starts that way. Let's see what the second syllable sounds like. One vowel again, and it's not at the end. That probably means a short sound for i, and c isn't followed by any letter, so I'll try the hard sound for that. That would be i, ti, tik. Plastik Oh, sure. Plastic! I'm surprised I didn't think of that right away because so many things are made of plastic.

Just described is a child who was not about to carry on a letter-by-letter analysis of plastic if it wasn't necessary, which is exactly right. To do so if it isn't necessary is to turn decoding into an end in itself when, in fact, it is supposed to be a means for achieving identifications. Because the spelling of plastic did not support either "leather" or "straw," this decoder temporarily moved away from the context to attend to visual cues. They suggested the syllables plas and tic. Consideration of syllabication stopped with the two syllables because the decoder was aware that every syllable must have a vowel sound; thus, no more than two were possible. He knew about letter-sound relationships and the features of syllables that signal information about likely sounds for vowels and for the consonant c. He also knew the correct way to blend sounds to form syllables.

To be sure that you know as much as this decoder did, let's move now to a detailed consideration of (a) letter-sound relationships, (b) factors that affect them, and (c) ways to use knowledge about both to decode words.

Letter-Sound Relationships

In an alphabetic writing system, letters stand for speech sounds. As was mentioned before, the letters associated with consonant sounds are referred to as consonants, while the letters that record vowel sounds are called vowels. Within that framework, y and w are consonants and vowels, since they record both consonant sounds (yes, want) and vowel sounds (oyster, owl).

Since the importance of vowel sounds for decoding has already been established (every syllable must have a vowel sound), let's start with them.

Vowel Sounds.   Earlier, the fifteen vowel sounds that figure in phonics instruction were identified. To see whether you remember them all, list below any fifteen words that could be used to illustrate all the sounds. Next, underline the letter or letters that record them.

————————————   ————————————   ————————————

————————————   ————————————   ————————————

————————————   ————————————   ————————————

————————————   ————————————   ————————————

————————————   ————————————   ————————————

Check your list with the one on page 36 to make certain that you accounted for all fifteen vowel sounds. (If you are unsure of any of the sounds, please study them before proceeding with the chapter, since subsequent pages assume you know them.)

Long Vowel Sounds. The five sounds in initial position in <u>age</u>, <u>eat</u>, <u>isle</u>, <u>ode</u>, and <u>use</u> have traditionally been referred to in phonics as *long* vowel sounds. They are identical to the names of five letters: <u>a</u>, <u>e</u>, <u>i</u>, <u>o</u>, <u>u</u>. (To help children keep conclusions about sounds in mind, diacritical marks are sometimes used: āgᴇ, ēat, īslᴇ, ōdᴇ, ūsᴇ.) A sixth vowel sound, heard in <u>ooze</u>, is the *long* sound for double-<u>o</u>. (Be sure you hear the distinction between the vowel sound in <u>use</u> [/yo͞o/] and the vowel sound in <u>ooze</u> [/o͞o/]. The two are closely similar, thus are easily confused. The first [/yo͞o/] is the long sound for <u>u</u>, and the second [/o͞o/] is the long sound for <u>oo</u>.)

Short Vowel Sounds. The five sounds heard initially in <u>at</u>, <u>end</u>, <u>ill</u>, <u>odd</u>, and <u>up</u> are referred to as *short* vowel sounds. The vowel sound in <u>good</u> is the short sound for <u>oo</u>. (Diacritical marks for the six short sounds are shown in ăt, ĕnd, ĭll, ŏdd, ŭp, go͝od).
 Since the short sound for double-o (to͝ok) is rare compared to the long sound (to͞ol), children should try the latter first whenever they are decoding a word in which adjacent <u>o</u>'s occur in a syllable. Eventually, they should know that the long sound for <u>oo</u> is sometimes represented by <u>u</u>, as in <u>blue</u>, <u>rule</u>, and <u>nutrition</u>.
 To help yourself hear the distinction between the long and short sounds for double-<u>o</u>, read the following contrasts aloud.

stool   fool   tool

stood   foot   took

Schwa Sound. A discussion of vowel sounds would be incomplete were the *schwa* sound bypassed. This is an unstressed sound that is closely similar to the short sound for **u**. It is symbolized in dictionaries by ə. If you'll take a minute now to glance through any dictionary, you will find frequent use of the schwa sound on every page. The frequency is accounted for by the fact that vowel sounds in unstressed syllables are commonly reduced to the schwa sound. To verify this, say *aloud* the words that are listed below; as you do, notice how each underlined letter, always in an unaccented syllable, stands for the schwa sound.

délta   aróma   síphon   offénse   húman

cónsonant   cemént   háven   búngalow

To make certain that you do hear the schwa sound, read the words below. Then underline all the vowel letters that stand for the schwa sound.

cellophane   condone   trophy   synthesize   maintain

typhoon   array   nomad   emblem   blaspheme.

Check what you selected with the Answer Key.

The schwa sound also figures in a type of syllable that was discussed earlier when generalizations for syllabicating unknown words were featured. I refer to the observation: When a word ends with a consonant followed by le, the three letters compose a syllable. How the schwa sound enters into this kind of syllable is illustrated below:

áble   púrple   búgle   dáwdle

a bəl   pur pəl   bu gəl   daw dəl

Additional Vowel Sounds. The three other vowel sounds that receive attention in phonics can be identified in the following words.

auto (or awe)   oil (or boy)   out (or owl)

The illustrations show how w and y function as vowels. Other times when y serves as a vowel will be described later.

A Summary. The lists of words in Table 3.4 will serve to review all the vowel sounds that have been discussed. Since they will continue to be referred to in the chapter, this is the time *to make certain* that you are familiar with them all.

Consonant Sounds. Most of the consonant sounds covered in phonics were identified earlier in the chapter, in the section called "Terminology." This is a good time to reread what was said about them.

"Special" Consonant Letters. As you reviewed the earlier material, you may have noticed that none of the seventeen words used to illustrate consonant sounds started with c, g, q, or x. Such words were omitted because the four letters require special attention. Decoders also have to give them special attention whenever they are found in unknown words.

C and g are "special" because each stands for two different sounds, referred to as the *hard* and *soft* sounds. The hard sound for c is the phoneme we usually associate with k.[4] It is heard in initial position in come, in medial position in act, and in final position in sac. The soft sound for c is the one we associate with s. It is heard initially in cent, cite, and cyst.

What is called the hard sound for g appears initially in go and game. It also occurs in final position in wag and drug. The

---

■ ■ **TABLE 3.4 Vowel Sounds**

Long Vowel Sounds heard in	Short Vowel Sounds heard in	Other Vowel Sounds heard in
ache	add	audit
ego	echo	ointment
idol	igloo	ouch
odor	odd	
unit	up *	
food	good	

* The schwa sound, you'll recall, is being equated with the short u sound.

---

[4] Even though we tend to think of /k/ in connection with k, it is a phoneme that is often recorded by other letters; for instance: cat, chord, pick, bouquet.

■ ■ **TABLE 3.5 Sounds Recorded by c and g**

	Hard Sounds	Soft Sounds
	/k/ cat	/s/ cell
	/g/ gull	/j/ gin

---

soft sound for g is the phoneme associated with j. It is heard once in gem and twice in ginger.

The two sounds for c and the two for g are summarized in Table 3.5.

When the hard and soft sounds for c and g are likely to occur will be discussed later in the section called "Factors That Affect Letter-Sound Relationships." For now, be sure you have all four sounds clearly in mind.

When special consonants are discussed, q cannot be overlooked. In this case, however, it is qu that merits attention, since the two letters function as if they were one consonant. In fact, when children see them in an unknown word, they should automatically think of qu as being a single consonant. Within that framework, qu records either a blend of two sounds (/kw/), as in queen, quest, and square, or a single sound (/k/), as in bouquet, clique, and unique. Typically, qu stands for /kw/ in initial position and for /k/ in final position.

To be noted, too, is that g, under certain circumstances, follows the pattern of q. That is, when g is followed by u in a syllable that has another vowel letter (e.g., guest, guide, vague), gu functions as if it were a single consonant. At such times, gu records the hard sound of g.

Still one more consonant requires special attention. I refer to x. Even though x records multiple sounds, it appears infrequently, thus causes few problems for decoders. Eventually they should know the following grapheme-phoneme correspondences,

---

■ ■ **TABLE 3.6 Sounds of x**

Phonemes	Examples
/ks/	fix, sox, axis
/gz/	exile, auxiliary
/z/	xerox, xylem

■ ■ **TABLE 3.7 Sounds Recorded by <u>th</u>**

Voiced Sound	*Voiceless Sound*
the	thin
either	ether
bathe	bath
thy	thigh

---

the first two of which occur more frequently than the third.

Sounds Recorded by Consonant Digraphs. In the discussion of terminology, six consonant digraphs and the sounds they represent were identified:

ph (phone)	sh (shell)	ng (rang)
gh (rough)	ch (chap, chef)	th (the, thin)

Since some people find it difficult to distinguish between the two sounds that <u>th</u> records in <u>the</u> and <u>thin</u>, I have listed some contrasts in Table 3.7 to maximize the difference between the two.

Reading the pairs aloud (e.g., <u>the</u>, <u>thin</u>) will help to emphasize the difference. Once you firmly fix in your mind the distinction between the voiced (<u>the</u>) and the voiceless sounds (<u>thin</u>), see whether you can put each of the following words under the correct classification.

there   them   thing   with   those   thumb   that

Voiced Sound   *Voiceless Sound*

Please check your decisions with the lists in the Answer Key.
As you did your classifying, one of your thoughts might have

been, "If *I'm* having trouble making distinctions, won't children really be puzzled?"

In this case, the distinction between the two sounds does not necessarily have to be made explicit for children, because they do what comes naturally. That is, when they say (think) the, them, there, that, and so on, they naturally use what phoneticians call a voiced sound at the beginning of each. And when they say or think words like thin, thumb, and thank, they naturally produce a voiceless sound. For teachers, however, hearing the distinction is essential if they are to avoid using a mixture of the two sounds when they are trying to illustrate one. Specifically, should they select the to illustrate a sound recorded by th, they should also refer to words such as them and there, but not to words like thin and thumb.

Unfortunately, commercially prepared materials (workbooks, for instance) sometimes use words like the and thumb to illustrate the same sound. The knowledgeable teacher bypasses such material, alters it, or, depending upon the ability of the children being taught, points out the error.

TESTING

Now that the vowel and consonant sounds have been identified, it is time for more testing. To start, see whether you can name the number of phonemes in each of the following words. The first has been done to serve as an example.

beet	tell	fault	stress
3 phonemes	__phonemes	__phonemes	__phonemes

pun	thin	guess	shine
__phonemes	__phonemes	__phonemes	__phonemes

brook	tax
__phonemes	__phonemes

Answers are in the Answer Key.

For the next part of the testing, six categories will be used:

1. *Words with Consonant Clusters*

2. *Words with Consonant Digraphs*

3. *Words with Short Vowel Sounds*

4. *Words with Long Vowel Sounds*

5. *Words with Soft Sound of C*

6. *Words with Hard Sound of G.*

The following words will also be used:

bathe	dust	glance	prince
broom	elm	king	seed
chop	foot	mouth	shame
cinch	gasp	phase	stood
clean	gaze	pool	thug

For this test, put under the first category all the words listed that have consonant clusters; under the second category, all those with consonant digraphs; and so on. (A word can be placed under more than one category.) After you make your lists, check them against those in the Answer Key. If making them was difficult, what has been covered thus far in the chapter should be reviewed.

Factors That Affect Letter-Sound Relationships

As was pointed out, some letters (e.g., a and g) stand for more than one sound. Since that is the case, how is a decoder to know what sound letters like these are representing in an unknown word? Commonly, (a) other letters in the same syllable plus (b) the order in which the letters occur provide hints, or cues, about the likely (not inevitable) sound. Exactly what those letters and sequences are is the concern now.

Vowel Sounds. As you know from your own experiences as a reader and speller, vowels show far more variation in the sounds they record than do consonants. In fact, the variability is the main reason most instructional programs in phonics start with consonant sounds. Fortunately, patterning does exist for vowels, and it is described in generalizations. Like others taught to decoders, these generalizations single out *visual* cues (letters and their sequence), since that is what's available to help when a word is not known. The generalizations also focus on syllables, not words. To say, for instance, that the sound that _a_ stands for is affected when _w_ follows it is based on the assumption that _a_ and _w_ are in the same syllable. The implication is that the sound for _a_ is affected by _w_ in _aw-ful_ (_aw ful_) but not in _aware_ (_a ware_).

Long and Short Vowel Sounds.   Several generalizations about long and short vowel sounds are listed in Table 3.8. As you

---

■ ■ **TABLE 3.8 Visual Cues for Long and Short Sounds**

When there is one vowel in a syllable and it is not in final position, it usually records its short sound. For example:

red   inch   accent   campus

When there is one vowel in a syllable and it is in final position, it usually records its long sound. For example:

I   she   polo   acne

When there are two adjacent vowels in a syllable and they are not a special digraph, the long sound of the first generally occurs.* For example:

coat   reel   maintain   eagle

When there are two vowels in a syllable, the second of which is final _e_, and the two are separated by one consonant, the first vowel generally stands for its long sound and the final _e_ is silent. For example:

pile   safe   vacate   stampede

When there are two vowels in a syllable, the second of which is final _e,_ and the two are separated by two consonants, the first vowel generally stands for its short sound and the final _e_ is silent. For example:

since   budge   expense   evolve

* The digraph _ow_ is an exception. Sometimes the sound it stands for follows the generalization (e.g., _own, window, borrow_); and sometimes it records the sound referred to earlier (e.g., _owl now, powder._) Children should try the long _o_ sound first. If that doesn't produce a recognizable word, the other sound should be used.

---

study them, be sure to keep in mind that the focus is syllables. That is, when you consider a multisyllabic word that is used to illustrate a generalization (e.g., <u>accent</u>), divide it into syllables with the help of generalizations discussed earlier in the chapter (<u>ac</u> <u>cent</u>). Then examine how one or more of the syllables exemplify the generalization.

Like other generalizations, those in Table 3.8 should be memorized once they are understood. (Understanding will be facilitated by comparing the five generalizations to see how their details vary.)

On the assumption that you understand and have memorized the generalizations, it's time for some testing.

TESTING

Consider the following nonsense words by, first, dividing them into syllables—if more than one exists. Next, under each word write all the generalizations that would be pertinent in deciding which vowel sound is likely to occur in each syllable.

1. <u>dreack</u>

____

____

____

2. <u>crodix</u>

____

____

3. <u>stadge</u>

____

4. <u>thade</u>

Please check your statements with those in the Answer Key to see whether the content (not necessarily the wording) of your generalizations matches what is there.

A Marker.   The nonsense words <u>stadge</u> and <u>thade</u> merit additional attention because they demonstrate the importance of final <u>e</u>'s for decoding.

When you analyzed <u>stadge</u>, you might have thought about the possibility of its being two syllables because of the two vowels, <u>a</u> and <u>e</u>. What should have kept you from dividing it was the final <u>e</u>, because final <u>e</u>'s almost never record a sound unless, of course, no other vowel is available to record the vowel sound that a syllable requires (e.g., <u>she</u>, <u>apostrophe</u>).

Although silent, final <u>e</u>'s assist decoders by signaling information about the likely sounds for other letters. In the case of <u>stadge</u>, for instance, <u>e</u> suggested a short sound for <u>a</u>, whereas in <u>thade</u> it suggested the long sound. In <u>stadge</u>, it also suggested the soft sound for <u>g</u>. When final <u>e</u> provides information about other letters, it is referred to as a *marker*.[5]

Flexible Application of Generalizations.   Like all other phonic generalizations, those about vowel sounds must be applied with flexibility. In working on an unknown word like <u>taste</u>, for instance, a decoder should try a short sound for <u>a</u> first, since that is the most likely sound. However, when it fails to yield anything sensible, the next step is to try the long sound, which does produce a real word.

---

[5] As was explained in the chapter on contextual cues, words are also markers, since they signal information about other words.

A type of word that often requires a switch from one vowel sound (long) to another (short) is illustrated below:

| solo | (so lo) | final | (fi nal) | motor | (mo tor) |
| solid | (so lid) | finish | (fi nish) | model | (mo del) |

As the various illustrations indicate, practice in manipulating sounds until a correct pronunciation is achieved merits much attention in instructional programs if they are to succeed in turning out proficient decoders. Such practice should always be carried on with unknown words that are in a context. Sentences like the following, for instance, might constitute an assignment in which children work out the pronunciation of the underlined words—all unfamiliar—with the help of contexts, spellings, and generalizations.

The <u>pedal</u> on the bike is broken.

A <u>spider</u> has eight legs.

They're sick with a <u>virus</u>.

I wish I had a <u>wagon</u> like yours.

The ice will soon be <u>solid</u>.

What exercises like these inevitably reveal is the dependence of successful decoding on oral vocabularies. More specifically, children who have never heard the word <u>solid</u> will be just as content with "sōlid" as with "sŏlid" because they have nothing stored in their auditory memories against which they can compare what they think the series of five letters might say. And it is just such comparisons that are at the core of the decoding process.

That oral vocabularies allow for shifts from approximately correct pronunciations to precisely correct ones is another point to bear in mind. How a shift might occur can be portrayed with more mind reading. This time, let's assume a decoder comes across <u>isolate</u> (which is unfamiliar visually) in the following sentence: <u>Their plan was to isolate one part of the army from the other.</u> Let's further assume that her thoughts resemble the following:

Let's see now. It's something they're going to do to the enemy to try to win. <u>S</u> has a vowel before and after it, so that makes <u>i</u> a syllable all by itself. <u>L</u> has a vowel before and after it, so that makes <u>s</u>, <u>o</u> another syllable. Gee, this is easy. Both those *syllables are words. Oh, and late is a word I know! Ī-sō-lāte. Oh, I know. Ĭ-sŭ-lāte. Sure, they're going to try to divide the army.*

The thoughts of the decoder just described allow for attention to three important points. First, as she demonstrated so successfully, syllabication, like isolation, is a way to divide and conquer. Second, it was her familiarity with the spoken form of isolate that allowed for the shift from an approximately correct pronunciation to the precisely correct one. And, third, the same familiarity allowed for an understanding of the meaning of the sentence—which, after all, is what reading is all about.

R-controlled Vowel Sounds. Whenever r follows a vowel in a syllable (e.g., arbor; ar bor), *r-controlled vowel sounds* result. In such instances, teachers should not specify for children what the vowel sound is. Instead, the vowel plus r should be treated as a unit, as should the blended sounds that the two letters stand for. A generalization about the blends that vowels plus r often record is stated below.

When r follows a vowel in a syllable, the vowel plus r often stands for one of three blends that are illustrated in her, for, and car.

The blend that e and r stand for in her is one that all the vowels plus r record: dollar, her, dirt, word, hurl. Consequently, if using the blends that are associated with ar (car) and or (for) fails to produce anything meaningful when ar or or occurs in an unknown word, the blend associated with er should be tried. Trying it will yield correct pronunciations for such words as custard, cedar, world, and stubborn. Infrequently, the blend associated with or (for) is represented by ar (e.g., war, dwarf, warden).

To sum up, a common pronunciation for a vowel plus r is the blend heard in her. Other possible blends are those occurring in car and for.

As was mentioned, a vowel sound is affected by r when r follows a vowel within a syllable. With that in mind, divide the following words into syllables by using visual cues that were specified earlier. Then decide whether or not each has an r-controlled vowel sound.

	Syllables	*R-Controlled Vowel Sounds*	
		Yes	No
1. burro	————	————	————
2. urchin	————	————	————
3. spiral	————	————	————
4. aroma	————	————	————
5. sorrow	————	————	————

First, check the Answer Key to see whether your syllabic divisions for the five words are correct. (If any are not, this is the time to review the generalizations for syllabicating words.) Next, see whether your decisions about r-controlled vowel sounds match those in the Answer Key. Finally, take the time to learn whether you can decode each of the five words using nothing but visual cues. What has been discussed thus far should allow you to do that; consequently, if you cannot, the generalizations dealing with vowel sounds need to be reviewed.

In thinking about vowel sounds and r, one other observation is necessary: When a vowel is followed in a syllable by re (e.g., dire, a ware), blends that can be identifield in the following words are common: care, mere, hire, more, sure. Contrasting words like those listed below are helpful for pointing out to children the different effects that r and re have on vowel sounds:

| fir | bar | her | cur | for |
| fire | bare | here | cure | fore |

What these and all other words clearly demonstrate is the relevance of the *whole* of a syllable for pronunciations. In fact, one lesson to be gleaned from the various generalizations about vowel sounds is the fundamental importance of examining all the letters in a syllable, plus their sequence, *before* tentatively choosing sounds for the letters. To illustrate, a decision should not be made about the pronunciation of a word starting with bo until the whole of the syllable in which bo appears has been scanned. The significance of the whole for pronunciations is clearly demonstrated in such words as box, boot, bone, bout, bore, and bow.

Y Functioning as a Vowel.   Do you recall being asked by one or more teachers, "What are the vowels?" And do you remember answering, "A, e, i, o, u, and sometimes y?" The reason for "and sometimes y" is that y often records vowel sounds. In fact, the consonant sound for y (yes, yard) occurs only when y starts a syllable; that is, is in initial position. The consonant sound, therefore, is in yam and yonder and also in canyon (can yon) and beyond (be yond). Knowing that the consonant sound only occurs in initial position is important when children work out unfamiliar words.

To illustrate the importance, let's assume hyssop is unfamiliar visually. Because identifying it requires knowing what sound to assign to y, a decoder has to decide whether y starts a syllable. If it does in hyssop, the division would be h yssop, which is impossible because every syllable must have a vowel sound. The implication, therefore, is that y is functioning as a vowel. Since it is, the correct syllabication is hys sop. (When two consonants [s and s] are preceded and followed by vowels [y and o], a syllabic division occurs between the consonants [hys sop].)

The need to know how y functions in an unknown word suggests it is time for more testing:

a. Divide each of the following words into syllables so that y is in initial position.

b. Based on the division, could y be a consonant?

	Syllabic Division If y Is a Consonant	Possible? Yes	No
1. type	_______________	______	______
2. symbol	_______________	______	______
3. myrtle	_______________	______	______
4. lawyer	_______________	______	______
5. fancy	_______________	______	______

Please check the Answer Key.

The letter that follows y in a word is another source of help when a decoder needs to know whether y is functioning as a consonant or a vowel. Specifically, if y is followed by a vowel, it is functioning as a consonant (e.g., lawyer). On the other hand, if y is followed by a consonant or occurs at the end of a word it is functioning as a vowel (e.g., type, symbol, myrtle, cry).

Now, knowing that y is functioning as a vowel in the four words listed below, divide each one into syllables using *visual* cues.

Syllabic Division

1. type _________________

2. symbol _________________

3. myrtle _________________

4. fancy _________________

Check your divisions with those in the Answer Key.

Using *auditory* cues (that is, what you hear when you say the words), describe what vowel sound y is recording in the same four words.

Vowel Sound
Recorded by y

1. type _________________

2. symbol _________________

3. myrtle _________________

4. fancy _________________

Again, please check your descriptions with the Answer Key.

Now that you know the vowel sounds that y can represent, please study the generalizations in Table 3.9, which pinpoint

---

■ ■ TABLE 3.9 Y Functioning as a Vowel

---

1. When y is in a syllable that has no other vowel and it is in medial position, it usually stands for the short i sound. For example:

   gym   myth   hyssop   syntax

2. When y records the final sound in a multisyllabic word, it usually represents the long e sound. For example:

   fancy   merry   plenty   autopsy

3. When y is the second of two adjacent vowels that are not a special digraph, it is silent. For example:

   say   pray   pulley   alley

4. Otherwise, y is most likely to stand for the long i sound. For example:

   by   dye   cycle   asylum   typhoon

---

when each sound is likely to occur. (Again, divide into syllables any multisyllabic word that illustrates a generalization before you consider how it does illustrate it.) Please study, *compare,* and then memorize the generalizations about y functioning as a vowel.

On the assumption that you understand and can repeat each generalization in Table 3.9, let's turn to more testing.

TESTING

a. Using the generalizations about syllabicating words, divide each nonsense word shown below into syllables. Assume in each case that y is functioning as a vowel.

b. After examining the type of syllable in which y occurs, write in the second column the number of the generalization (see Table 3.9) that suggests what sound y records.

	Syllables	*Number of Generalization*
1. slonny	———————	————
2. brayno	———————	————
3. slym	———————	————
4. pryple	———————	————
5. slyte	———————	————
6. oyton	———————	————

Please check the Answer Key, first to see about the syllabic divisions and then about the generalization chosen for each word.

This brings to a close the discussion of vowel letters and the sounds they represent. Since the importance of vowel sounds for decoding should now be obvious, this is a good time to reread (and, if necessary, restudy) the whole of the discussion. As you do, remember that only when teachers know something well can their instruction about it be effective.

Consonant Sounds. Typically, attention to some consonant sounds constitutes beginning phonics instruction. Choosing consonants rather than vowels at the start is sensible, since the speech sounds that consonants represent are fairly consistent from word to word. To teach all the consonant sounds before any attention goes to vowel sounds would not make sense, however, for two reasons. First, some consonants rarely occur in words; and, second, vowel sounds are extremely important because every syllable has one.

Sounds Recorded by Digraphs. Even though consonants *are* fairly consistent in the sounds they stand for, some require special attention. Those that form digraphs fall into that category:

th (then; thorn)	ph (phrase)	ch (church; chalet)
sh (shut)	gh (tough)	ng (long)

As has already been mentioned, the six digraphs shown

above must be treated by decoders as if they were a single consonant, because each stands for a sound that is unlike the sound associated with either letter making up the pair. You will also recall that these special digraphs function as a single consonant when unknown words are being syllabicated:

ether (e ther)   orchard (or chard)   typhoon (ty phoon)

Hard and Soft Sounds for C and G.   C and g also need special consideration, for each stands for two different sounds. As was explained earlier, the two are referred to as *hard* and *soft* sounds.

To see whether you recall the two, describe the sounds that c and g represent in the following words by placing a check in the appropriate column.

	Hard Sound	*Soft Sound*
1. angry	_______	_______
2. splice	_______	_______
3. success	_______	_______
4. gentle	_______	_______
5. emerge	_______	_______

Please check the Answer Key. (If you are unsure of the four sounds, return to the earlier part of the chapter where they are described.)

The generalization that helps a decoder make decisions about sounds for c and g is stated below. What it does is point to markers; that is, to letters that signal information about c and g.

When c and g are followed in a syllable by e, i, or y, they generally stand for their soft sounds. Otherwise, the hard sounds are common. For example:

| city | ounce | cyst | wage | gym | ginger |
| can't | climb | picnic | wag | gum | argue |

TESTING

Using what has now been said about (a) syllabication, (b) letter-sound relationships, and (c) factors that affect them, examine the list of words below to see whether they are regularly spelled.[6] To do that:

a. Divide each word into syllables using the visual cues that are described in phonic generalizations.
b. Consider each syllable in a word to see whether its pronunciation corresponds to what one or more of the generalizations predict. If the pronunciation of all of its syllables does match predictions, mark the word as being regularly spelled. If one or more of its syllables has a pronunciation that is not predicted, mark it irregularly spelled.
c. For each irregularly spelled word, give a spelling that makes it regularly spelled. Use no diacritical marks—just letters.

	Regularly Spelled?		(If not)
	Yes	No	Regular Spelling
shoe		X	shoo
sym/bol	X		
1. trauma			
2. buffalo			
3. once			
4. sauce			
5. textile			
6. torpedo			
7. urge			

[6] For this exercise, "regularly spelled" means that the pronunciation of the word is predictable from the generalizations that have been highlighted in the chapter. One prediction, you'll recall, is that vowel sounds in unstressed syllables are commonly reduced to the schwa sound.

| | Regularly Spelled? | | (If not) |
	Yes	No	Regular Spelling
8. wolf	_______	_______	_____________
9. thread	_______	_______	_____________
10. gargle	_______	_______	_____________
11. finance	_______	_______	_____________
12. vaccine	_______	_______	_____________
13. mourn	_______	_______	_____________
14. among	_______	_______	_____________
15. volcano	_______	_______	_____________
16. flood	_______	_______	_____________
17. accent	_______	_______	_____________
18. sympathy	_______	_______	_____________

Before checking the Answer Key, make certain that:
a. You divided each word into syllables using visual cues that are described in phonic generalizations.
b. You remembered that a schwa sound in an unstressed syllable does not make a word irregularly spelled.
c. You changed the fewest letters possible when you provided a regular spelling for an irregularly spelled word.
Now check the Answer Key.

Stressed Syllables

As you worked on the list of words in order to see whether any were irregularly spelled, you knew which syllable to stress in all the multisyllabic words because you can read them. However, what about children who cannot read a word of more than one syllable and who have to work out what a multisyllabic word says? How will they know which syllable to stress once they decide that the word *is* multisyllabic? To respond, some basic points about decoding need to be reviewed.

1. Decoding provides meaningful help to readers only when they know the words in their spoken form. This is the case even with regularly spelled, single-syllable words. To illustrate, <u>auk</u> is readily decodable, but what good is it for a reader to know its pronunciation if its meaning is a mystery?

2. When a word (e.g., <u>acquaint</u>) is visually unfamiliar but is known in its spoken form, readers can match what decoding produces (ăc kwā/nt) with what is stored in their auditory memories (ə kwā/nt) and, as a result, shift from an approximately correct to a precisely correct pronunciation. To be remembered is that such adjustments are facilitated not only by oral vocabularies but also by contextual cues.

What should now be clear is that teachers can make substantial contributions to children's decoding abilities by doing whatever is possible to extend their experiences and concepts and the vocabulary that goes with both. For decisions about stressed syllables, they can contribute still more by giving children practice in manipulating stress. Starting with words children are able to read, teachers themselves can model—thus explain—manipulation with pronunciations like the following, in which stress is given to each successive syllable starting with the first one:

<u>picture</u>   <u>torpedo</u>

pic/ture   pic túre   tór pe do   tor pé do   tor pe dó

Once children acquire facility in varying stress in familiar words (this helps explain the job to be done), teachers can next demonstrate how manipulation helps achieve the correct identification of a word that is not familiar.

How children can try out stress is portrayed below with the thoughts of another decoder. This time the puzzling word is <u>establish</u>, which is in the sentence <u>The family wanted to establish a home there.</u>

I wonder if this is a word that means something like "find" or "get" or "have." I don't think I've ever seen it before. It's a

verb—a long verb, that's for sure. I'd better divide it. Two consonants with a vowel before and after them probably mean that e, s is the first syllable. There are two more consonants with vowels before and after them, so that probably means the three syllables are e, s; t, a, b; and l, i, s, h. Let's see what their sounds are. Oh, they're all the same. One vowel and it's not at the end. So that would be: es-tab-lish. Establish? I can't think of any word that sounds like that. Let's see what happens if I stress the first syllable. Establish. I never heard of that. Let's try the next syllable. Estáblish. Oh, sure, establish. That means to start—like starting a business. I guess here it means the family wants to start having a home. No wonder. They sure have been on the move.

■ ■ What Decoders Need to Be Able to Do

What children must know about (a) syllabication, (b) letter-sound relationships, and (c) the factors that affect them has now been dealt with. However, as the thoughts of the decoder just described demonstrated, knowing is not enough. Readers also have to be able to use what they know. In other words, they have to be able to *do* certain kinds of things. With that requirement in mind, it is time to shift the focus to a discussion of how the content of phonics is used with unknown words.

Before the shift is made, one point needs to be underscored: Even though the content of phonics was discussed in one section of the chapter and how it is used is to be discussed now, the division should not lead you to incorrectly conclude that an instructional program covers content first, then its use Correctly viewed, instruction deals with a little content, then how it is used; with a little more content and how that is used; and so on. Whenever necessary, reviews and reteaching enter into the cycle, too.

Use Initial Letters and Sounds

How children begin to use what they know about symbols and sounds to identify words was described in Chapter 2. You will recall, for example, that knowledge of just a few consonant sounds allows for practice in supplying missing words in written contexts when only their first letter is provided. Because of the close connection between practice with contextual cues and early use of graphophonic cues, it is advisable that you at least skim the earlier chapter and also review Table 2.1.

Use Phonemic Additions and Substitutions

Later use of symbols and sounds to identify words involves *phonemic additions* and *phonemic substitutions*. (These processes should be introduced only when letter-sound relationships are known at the automatic level. Premature use requires a child to think about too many things at once.) Of the five possible processes (adding beginning sound; adding final sound; substituting beginning sound; substituting final sound; substituting medial sound), adding a final sound to a known word in order to achieve the identification of an unknown one is the easiest. This is the case because all children have to do is say the word they know (e.g., an), then say it again, this time adding another sound (e.g., /t/) to the end. The result is the identification of the unfamiliar word (ant). Further examples of final phoneme additions are in Table 3.10.

Once children understand what adding sounds to the ends of words means and, in addition, understand how such additions help with unknown words, they are ready for practice in adding sounds to the beginning of words. A teacher who demonstrates the new process as a way of explaining it will write something like the following on a chalkboard. (In each instance, the top word is one the children can read, whereas the one underneath is new.)

at	our	and	it	park
sat	sour	sand	sit	spark

■ ■ **TABLE 3.10 Examples of Final Phoneme Additions**

Known Word	Unknown Word	Final Addition
car	card	/d/
ten	tent	/t/
paw	pawn	/n/
bus	bust	/t/
mar	marsh	/sh/

The teacher begins by modeling; that is, by reading the pairs of words aloud in order to show what adding a sound to the beginning of a word means. Eventually, how initial and final phoneme additions function together should be pointed out. For example, if scant, scarf, and Scotch are unfamiliar, initial and final additions like those shown below can be demonstrated:

can	car	cot
scan	scar	Scot
scant	scarf	Scotch

Thus far, only phoneme additions have been illustrated. Tables 3.11 and 3.12 list examples of phoneme substitutions.

With very few exceptions (e.g., ant→act), medial substitutions involve vowel sounds (man→men; sit→sat; cub→cab). Medial substitutions are the most difficult for children to make; they should not be introduced, therefore, until proficiency in adding and substituting phonemes in initial and final positions is achieved.

■ ■ **TABLE 3.11 Initial Phoneme Substitutions**

Known Word	Unknown Word	Substitution
fast	past	/p/ for /f/
lip	zip	/z/ for /l/
lamp	champ	/ch/ for /l/
in	an	/ă/ for /ĭ/

■ ■ **TABLE 3.12 Final Phoneme Substitutions**

Known Word	Unknown Word	Substitution
if	in	/n/ for /f/
art	arc	/k/ for /t/
fit	fish	/sh/ for /t/
he	hi	/ī/ for /ē/

Although practice with additions and substitutions is initiated with single syllable words, they also function with multisyllabic words:

stable dribble deacon limber battle   number aroma

staple drizzle beacon slumber saddle cucumber arena

To sum up, all the following processes in Table 3.13 are available to help children use (a) known words and (b) letter-sound relationships to decode unknown words.

While it is easy to list the processes, it is much more difficult for children to use them. And this will be the case even when teachers provide ample instruction and practice. The difficulty reflects the fact that using the processes involves more than might be apparent. More specifically, to use the known word <u>but</u> to help with the unknown word <u>bus</u> requires ability to do the following:

1. Recall <u>but</u> at the time <u>bus</u> is encountered

2. Recognize its similarity to <u>bus</u>

3. Remember the sound that <u>s</u> represents

4. Substitute that sound for /t/ in final position

These requirements suggest the need for teachers to frequently ask children, "What word do you know that looks something like this new word?" Written exercises like the following should also be provided. In this case, words children can read are placed in parentheses, while the new words are underscored.

<u>Stan</u> is his name.   (can)

Put the horse in the <u>stable</u>.   (table)

■ ■ **TABLE 3.13 Phoneme Additions and Substitutions**

Unknown Word	Known Word	Helpful Process
sand	and	Initial Addition
bunch	bun	Final Addition
chalk	talk	Initial Substitution
trait	train	Final Substitution
fin	tun	Medial Substitution

The <u>brook</u> runs through the farm.   (book)

She had on a yellow <u>blouse</u>.   (house)

More advanced practice omits the known words. Now, children receive directions like: "All the words that are underlined are new. For each one, try to think of a word you know that looks something like it. When you've decided what the underlined word says, write a sentence using it. That way I'll know whether you figured it out correctly."

Written practice like that just described not only provides for independent work that is relevant for decoding but also allows for the reminder that contextual cues should not be overlooked even when the concentration is on graphophonic cues. Contexts are especially important when the children's phoneme additions and substitutions fail to lead directly to a meaningful word, as in the following sentences:

A <u>dome</u> is on top of the church.   (come)

I need a <u>pint</u> of cream.   (pin)

My <u>shoe</u> is much too tight.   (toe)

The bears are in the <u>cave</u>.   (have)

Put that <u>bowl</u> on the table, please.   (owl)

Try Out Sounds

In addition to knowing how to use the help that derives from contexts, children should also be prepared to try more than one sound (especially for vowel letters) whenever the initial use of letter-sound relationships, or of phoneme additions and substitutions, fails to produce the correct word. To illustrate, when decoders realize that <u>come</u> does not provide direct help with the pronunciation of <u>dome</u>, they should substitute other sounds for <u>o</u> starting with /ō/, since that sound is suggested in a generalization. In this instance, the first try works. With <u>shoe</u>, on the other hand, greater effort is required. After recognizing that <u>toe</u> does not lead directly to anything that is sensible in the given context, decoders should next try /ŏ/, which doesn't help either. The next job, therefore, is to try still more vowel sounds until one (/ōō/) yields a word that makes sense in <u>My shoe is much too tight</u>.

Blend Phonemes

In addition to being able to use contexts and phoneme additions and substitutions in flexible ways, children also need to know how to blend phonemes to produce syllables. When they first encounter a word like elf, for instance, they should be able to conclude from visual cues that it is one syllable and that e probably represents /ĕ/. They should also know how to combine /ĕ/, /l/, and /f/ and thus achieve the pronunciation of elf. Since elf starts with a vowel, the sequence of the blending follows the sequence of the three letters:

$$\breve{e} \rightarrow \breve{e}l \rightarrow \breve{e}lf$$

Just as trying out sounds was seen to be an advanced use of phoneme substitutions, so blending sounds to produce syllables should be seen as an advanced use of phoneme additions. Further examples of blending follow, presented as they would be shown to children:

awl	else	ounce	east	act
aw	ĕ	ou	ēa	ă
awl	ĕl	oun	ēas	ăc
	ĕlse	ounce	ēast	ăct

As might already be apparent, blending sounds is not the quickest way to achieve identifications. If a child knew fact, for example, omitting /f/ would be the most efficient procedure for identifying act. Since it has to be assumed, however, that related words will not always be known or, if known, will not always be recalled, children do need to know how to blend phonemes—just in case.

When blending phonemes is required for a syllable whose initial letter is a consonant, it is best to start with the first vowel sound, to which the initial consonant sound can then be added. From that point on, blending follows the sequence of the remaining letters. For instance:

pŏnd	sharp	bāke	ăl cōve
ŏ	ar	ā	ă ō
pŏ	shar	bā	ăl cō
pŏn	sharp	bāke	cōve
pŏnd			

For another illustration of blending, see the earlier description of a decoder's thoughts on page 44.

Why a special sequence is recommended for words or syllables that start with consonants has to do with the inevitable distortion of consonant sounds when they are produced alone; that is, apart from syllables. The distortion is especially acute for *stop sounds:*

$$/b/ \qquad /p/$$
$$/d/ \qquad /t/$$
$$/g/ \qquad /k/$$

Isolating any of the stop sounds results in a distortion that could be described as the sound of the consonant combined with /ŭ/. An attempt to produce /b/, for example, results in a blend of two sounds that is spelled <u>buh</u>. That is why synthesizing the sounds that compose a word like <u>bad</u> in the sequence suggested by its letters is likely to result in "buh-ad." While some children can shift from "buh-ad" to "bad," others cannot. To help the latter, the recommendation is to teach the following: Blend phonemes in the sequence suggested by the letters composing a syllable whenever it starts with a vowel (ă→ăc→ăct). Start with the first vowel sound in a syllable whenever it begins with one or more consonants (ă→bă→băd).

TESTING

Let's assume that you subscribe to the guideline just mentioned and, further, that you want to display blending sequences for children. With that in mind, write the sequences for blending phonemes to produce the words shown below. The first has been done to serve as an example.

ten	church	ilk	cuff	pawn	each	cube
ĕ						
tĕ						
tĕn						

Please check your sequences and diacritical marks with what is in the Answer Key. Afterwards, read aloud each sequence for each word just as you would do were you modeling blending for children.

Although the discussion and testing of phoneme blending pointed out every possible step, it should be remembered that skilled decoders often leap to pronunciations. Having divided alcove into its two syllables, for instance, and having made tentative decisions about the likely sounds for the letters that compose each one, a skilled decoder would automatically know the pronunciation of each syllable. (See page 67 for an example of this kind of automaticity.) It is also likely, however, that the same decoder went through earlier stages in blending in which small steps, like those portrayed earlier, were taken. Teachers must be sufficiently knowledgeable to be able to guide children through those early steps using, at the start, some short, one-syllable words. Like other instruction concerned with the use of what is taught in phonics, this will begin with the teacher modeling the procedure.

A Summary

As was mentioned earlier in the chapter on contexts, children need to be able to use minimal spellings, plus contexts, to arrive at pronunciations. Minimal spellings are often sufficient when new words are embedded in contexts that are rich with both syntactic and semantic cues.

If children's reading vocabularies include words that bear a phonic relationship to unfamiliar words, children also need to be able to recall the known words and to use them (along with phoneme additions and substitutions) to learn what the new words say. If additions and substitutions fail to achieve meaningful words, the children have to be ready to try out alternative sounds (especially for vowels) until a sensible word is produced.

Finally, children need to be able to apply generalizations dealing with syllabication, letter-sound relationships, and factors that affect them. Such application is necessary because it is the starting point whenever an unfamiliar word has to be figured out letter by letter and syllable by syllable. Whenever that is the case, children have to be able to blend phonemes to produce a word or syllable. With a multisyllabic word, they also have to know how to manipulate stress until they achieve the correct pronunciation.

Not to be forgotten is the value of an approximately correct pronunciation, for it is often sufficient to suggest the correct one. Not to be overlooked, either, is a point that was made repeatedly in the chapter: All uses of graphophonic cues are facilitated by children's oral vocabularies.

USE OF STRUCTURAL ANALYSIS TO IDENTIFY WORDS

Terminology

What Is Taught for Structural Analyses

A Summary

What Children Need to Be Able to Do
  to Use Structural Cues

Etymology

Were you to reread the previous chapter, you would see that all the words that illustrated generalizations and that figured in explanations of decoding strategies are roots. For instance, success and author were used as examples, but successful and authors were not. Words like successful and authors were deliberately omitted because what is taught in phonics is meant to help with roots. On the other hand, what is taught under the topic "Structural Analysis" is about derived and inflected words.

Before the discussion of structural analysis gets under way, *root, derived word,* and *inflected word* will be defined, since they enter into the discussion frequently.

■ ■ Terminology

To help with the definitions, the list below starts with a term that is more encompassing than the others; namely, *word family.*

Word family.   A group of related words whose roots are either identical (call, caller, recall, uncalled, etc.) or of the same origin (inspect, spectacles, spectator, inspector, etc.).

Root.   The smallest unit in which the meaning shared by the members of a family exists. Call, for example, is a root. (Reducing call to all is a phonic rather than a structural reduction, since all is not a family member.)

Base.   A synonym for *root.*

Prefix.   A unit of one of more letters placed before a root to form a word with a different meaning than the root. Examples of prefixes added to roots are preschool, amoral, disobey, and reread.

Suffix.   A unit of one or more letters added to the end of a root that affects its meaning or grammatical function. Suffixes are of two kinds: derivational and inflectional.

Derivational suffix.   A unit of one or more letters added to the end of a root to form a word with a different meaning than the root. Examples of derivational suffixes added to roots are point<u>less</u>, cap<u>ful</u>, care<u>free</u> and play<u>able</u>.

Inflectional suffix. A unit of one or more letters added to the end of a root to form a word that retains the inherent meaning of the root but alters its grammatical function: changes its number, gender, tense, or voice; indicates possession or comparison; or changes an adjective to an adverb. Examples of inflectional suffixes added to roots are work<u>ed</u>, lamp<u>s</u>, cry<u>ing</u>, poor<u>ly</u> and soft<u>er</u>. *Inflection* is a synonym for inflectional suffix.

Inflected word. A word composed of a root plus an inflectional suffix. Examples are <u>treated</u>, <u>warmest</u>, <u>porches</u>, and <u>reading</u>.

Derived word. A word composed of a root and a prefix (<u>re-read</u>); a root and a derivational suffix (<u>homeless</u>); or a root, a prefix, and a derivational suffix (<u>unquenchable</u>). *Derivative* is a synonym for derived word.

Affix. A prefix or suffix.

Compound word. A word composed of two or more roots. Examples are <u>nevertheless</u>, <u>lifelong</u>, <u>chairperson</u>, and <u>railroad</u>.

Before you review the definitions in preparation for a test, you might want to examine the lists in Table 4.1 since they sort out some of the terms.

Yet another way to organize some of the terms is shown in Table 4.2.

Once you have studied all the definitions that were given at the start of the chapter, please complete the following tests.

■ ■ **TABLE 4.1 Terminology for Structural Analysis**

Root (Base)	Derived Word (Derivative)	Inflected Word	Compound Word
name	nameless	named	namesake
hair	hairy	hairs	hairbrush
draw	redraw	drawing	drawbridge
button	unbutton	buttons	buttonhole

■ ■ **TABLE 4.2 Comparison of Terms**

Derived Word (Derivative)	Inflected Word	Compound Word
root + prefix	root + inflectional suffix (inflection)	root + root
root + derivational suffix		
root + prefix and derivational suffix		

TESTING

Indicate whether each of the statements below is true or false.

__________ 1. A word family is composed of a root plus derived and inflected words.

__________ 2. There are two kinds of suffixes, derivational and grammatical.

__________ 3. If two roots can be found in a word's spelling, it is a compound word.

__________ 4. Words like <u>rain</u>, <u>train</u>, and <u>strain</u> are members of the same family.

__________ 5. <u>Dictionary</u>, <u>dictation</u>, <u>indict</u>, and <u>dictator</u> are members of the same family.

__________ 6. A prefix is an affix, but it is not an inflection.

__________ 7. The word <u>ceaselessly</u> is a derivative.

Please check your judgments with the Answer Key. Afterwards, see how well you can do on the next test.

Match the terms in column one with the examples in column two by placing appropriate numbers in the parentheses.

1. derivational suffix   (   ) ly
2. root   (   ) barrels
3. inflected word   (   ) star
4. base   (   ) drawbridge
5. derivative   (   ) ment
6. prefix   (   ) mice
7. inflectional suffix   (   ) maltreat
8. derived word   (   ) il
9. inflection   (   ) nameless
10. compound word

Please check your responses with the Answer Key. If one test or both caused problems, this is the time to restudy the definitions. The rest of the chapter proceeds on the assumption that you understand all the terms that were defined.

■ ■ What Is Taught for Structural Analyses

As was suggested in the opening paragraph of the chapter and in the definitions that followed, instruction about word structure concentrates on prefixes, inflectional suffixes, and derivational suffixes. What children need to know about all three will be dealt with first. What they need to be able to do to turn their knowledge into the ability to work out the pronunciation and meaning of derived and inflected words will be discussed afterwards.

Sequence for Instruction

Assuming that it can be sorted out, the root of an inflected or a derived word may be one that children know. This puts them in the desirable position of being able to use what is known to deal with what is not. Separating out roots to learn whether they *are* familiar is easier if they appear first. Seeing read in reader, reading, and readable, for example, is easier than finding it in preread and reread.[1]

[1] At one time, hyphens usually separated prefixes from roots, making both the root and the prefix apparent. This practice is much less common now.

That roots are more apparent when the affix is a suffix than when it is a prefix explains why some inflectional and derivational suffixes are introduced before any attention goes to prefixes.

Inflectional Suffixes

Inflectional suffixes get attention before any goes to derivational suffixes because inflected words appear in reading materials earlier than derived words. In this discussion they will be referred to as inflections, since that is the term used eventually with children.

Typically, the first inflected words that children encounter are plural nouns, singular verbs, and past tense verbs—words like toys. runs, and played. From the start, children should be helped to understand how inflections like -s and -ed affect both the pronunciation and the meaning of roots. (Unlike phonic analyses, those concerned with structure help with meaning as well as with pronunciation. This makes structural analysis particularly valuable for readers.)

As was mentioned before, inflections signal information about grammatical function. More specifically, they indicate number, gender, or possession, if the root is a noun (e.g., books, lioness, child's); tense and voice if the root is a verb (e.g., worked, eaten); and comparison, if the root is an adjective or abverb (e.g., bigger, slowest). Adjectives (quick) can also be changed to adverbs (quickly) with the addition of an inflection.

Because inflections signal information, they are sometimes referred to as *markers,* a term that you were first introduced to in the chapter on contexts. In cars, the final s is a plural marker; in parked, -ed is a tense marker.

How nouns, verbs, adjectives, and adverbs can be inflected is further illustrated in Table 4.3.

Recognizing a known root in an inflected word helps decoders decide what the latter says and means. The easiest inflected words to deal with, therefore, are those in which the spelling of the familiar root remains intact. For instance:

toys	porches	played	acting	greener	slowly	fallen
toy	porch	play	act	green	slow	fall

That alterations in a root's spelling make it more difficult to recognize the root is illustrated on the next page under the table.

■ ■ **TABLE 4.3 Examples of Inflectional Suffixes**

Root	*Inflected Words*
door	doors
box	boxes
cherry	cherries
host	hosts, hostess, hostesses
girl	girl's, girls'
call	calls, called, calling, caller
dry	dries, dried, drying
watch	watches, watched, watching
prove	proves, proved, proving, proven
sweet	sweeter, sweetest
dry	drier, driest
thin	thinner, thinnest
soft	softly
gentle	gently
fast	faster
busy	busily

cities	smiled	funny	bravest	scary	taking	lazily
city	smile	fun	brave	scare	take	lazy

To help children decide what the root is when its spelling is altered, the generalizations listed in Table 4.4 should be taught. If any are unfamiliar, this is the time to study (memorize) them.

Once you can verbalize the generalizations, you are ready for the next test. (As was mentioned in the chapter on phonics, being able to state generalizations is important because the ability to put into words what needs to be communicated to children is a prerequisite for successful instruction.)

For each group of inflected words, starting with those following Table 4.4, state the generalization that accounts for their spelling.

■ ■ **TABLE 4.4 Generalizations That Are Helpful in Sorting Out Roots in Inflected and Derived Words**

The plural of nouns ending in f is formed by changing f to v and adding es. For instance:

calf	loaf
calves	loaves

When a root ends in a consonant followed by y, y is changed to i before adding es, ed, er, est, ly, ful, less, or ous. For instance:

duty	try	holy	tiny
duties	tried	holier	tiniest
merry	plenty	penny	melody
merrily	plentiful	penniless	melodious

When a root ends in a consonant that is preceded by a single vowel, the consonant is usually doubled before ed, er, ing, or y is added. For instance:

rob	run	wrap	mud
robbed	runner	wrapping	muddy

When a root ends in silent e, the e is usually omitted when an inflectional or derivational suffix beginning with a vowel is added. For instance:

brake	race	hate	excite
braking	racer	hated	excitable
	strange	rate	bride
	stranger	ration	bridal

1. calves, shelves, scarves, elves

Generalization: _______________________________

____

____

2. <u>barred, fitted, hitter, canning</u>

Generalization: ________________________________

____

____

3. <u>making, coded, driver, scenic</u>

Generalization: ________________________________

____

____

4. <u>busily, happiest, buried, drier</u>

Generalization: ________________________________

____

____

Examining the four groups of inflected words should have demonstrated how the generalizations will help children sort out roots when their spellings have been changed in an inflected or derived word. Now that you *have* examined them, check your four statements with the Answer Key. Wording need not exactly match what appears there; however, no important detail should be omitted.

Instruction with inflections should reflect the fact that children need to know (a) how they are pronounced, (b) how they affect syllabication, and (c) how they affect the grammatical function of roots. As a result of instruction with <u>-ly</u>, for instance, children should know how to pronounce it, how it adds a syllable to a root, and how it affects the root's grammatical function. More specifically, if they are familiar with <u>slow</u> and they come across <u>slowly</u> in their reading, they should know how to pronounce the inflected word and they should also understand how <u>-ly</u> has changed the adjective they know into an adverb.

Generalizations that should be taught because they help achieve the goals of instruction are in Table 4.5.

■ ■ **TABLE 4.5 Generalizations about Suffixes, Pronunciation, and Syllabication**

When -es forms a plural noun or a present tense verb, it is pronounced /əz/ and it adds an unstressed syllable to the root. For instance:

box	dish	bus	march	pass
boxes	dishes	buses	marches	passes

When the inflection -ed is affixed to a verb ending in d or t, it is an unstressed syllable that is pronounced /əd/. Otherwise, -ed adds a sound to the root (/d/ or /t/) but not a syllable. For instance:

last	add	seal	pass
lasted	added	sealed	passed

When -ion is affixed to a root whose final sound is /t/, the letters tion (not ion) compose the last syllable. Usually, tion is pronounced /shun/. For instance:

act	abduct	create
action	abduction	creation

Another Decoder's Thoughts

Before the focus shifts from inflectional to derivational suffixes, let's get inside the head of another decoder, whose strategies for dealing with flooding allow for a review of what has been said in this and the two previous chapters. That is, they demonstrate:

1. Using a context
2. Sorting out the root in an inflected word
3. Blending phonemes
4. Trying out vowel sounds until a recognizable word results

In this instance, the unknown word flooding occurs in the sentence Flooding is what they're afraid of.

This names whatever they're afraid of. i, n, g probably is an inflection. That leaves f, l, o, o, d for the root. That's easy:

ōō→flōō→flōōd. Flōōd? I don't think that's even a word. I better try the other sound for oo: ŏŏ→flŏŏ→flŏŏd. Flŏŏd? That's not a word either![2] I better try different vowel sounds: flăd, flĕd,[3] flŏd, flŭd—oh, now I know what it says. Flooding! They're afraid their basements will get flooded.

Derivational Suffixes

Some of the derivational suffixes that are taught initially are listed in Table 4.6. Instruction with any of these derivational suffixes starts with familiar roots (which in this case are nouns), then shows how they can be changed to descriptive words by adding certain letters. If children can read rain, curl, and milk, and -y is the derivational suffix selected for attention, the following words would be displayed on a chalkboard, arranged

---

■ ■ **TABLE 4.6 Some Common Derivational Suffixes**

Suffix	Meanings	Derivative
-y	full of; characterized by	rainy
-ful		careful
-ous		joyous
-less	without; free from	spotless
-able	capable of being	readable
-ward	in the direction of	homeward
-ly	like; pertaining to	saintly
-ic		heroic
-ish		foolish
-like		lifelike
-ive		excessive
-ative		talkative

---

[2] It's very possible that the wrong pronunciations are close enough to the right one to suggest what the word is, especially if prior sentences in the text offer semantic help. For our purposes let's assume the reader is still unable to identify *flood,* thus must try more alternatives.

[3] Trying /ē/ does produce a word, you'll notice, but not one that makes sense in the given context.

as shown in order to make apparent both the known root and the new suffix. (What is new should always be compared to what is known and related.)

rain   curl   milk

rainy   curly   milky

Once children know the pronunciation of -y and understand its semantic effect on roots with the help of the three (or more) pairs of words, they are ready to apply those learnings to other derivatives in which, again, the root is familiar. Now, words like roomy, cloudy, lucky, and chilly can be placed in contexts so that the children can decide how they are pronounced and what they mean. Later, derivatives with unfamiliar roots should be featured so that the children will see how graphophonic and structural cues function together.

With the help of the spelling generalizations that were referred to earlier in the chapter, the same children will eventually have to learn that spellings are altered when -y is affixed to certain kinds of roots. For example:

fun	mud	scare	juice
funny	muddy	scary	juicy

What must also be called to their attention so as to discourage overgeneralizing is that not all words ending in y are derivatives. Again, known words are helpful:

happy   story   candy   many   hurry   merry

Whether instruction with -y (or any other derivational suffix) is truly productive depends on what children are able to do when they come across an unfamiliar derivative—one like stony, for instance. If they are able (a) to conclude that the root is stone; (b) to decode it and, as a result, recognize it as a word they know in its spoken form; and (c) to arrive at both the pronunciation and meaning of stony, clear evidence exists that instruction was relevant and productive for reading.

Table 4.7 comprises other derivational suffixes that, if taught well, are helpful to readers. All indicate an agent; that is, someone who is occupied with whatever is indicated by the root. Since derivatives formed with -er show up in materials first, it is dealt with before the others. Again, known roots (e.g., play, work, walk, jump) provide a beginning for the instruction. At some point, instruction should contrast the function of -er in words like reader, harder, and faster; and it should also

---

■ ■ **TABLE 4.7 Suffixes Indicating an Agent**

Suffix	Noun	Suffix	Noun
-er	teacher	-ist	organist
-or	actor	-eer	auctioneer
-ar	liar	-ster	truckster

---

demonstrate that not all words ending in <u>er</u> are derivatives of roots. Words like <u>ever</u>, <u>rather</u>, <u>after</u>, and <u>finger</u> will help by showing that when <u>er</u> is removed, a root is not left.

Still more derivational suffixes are in Table 4.8. Because the derivatives they form, as well as their own meanings, are difficult to understand, instruction with these suffixes is postponed until common, easily understood prefixes have been dealt with.

Another Decoder's Thoughts

Before the discussion turns to prefixes, let's get inside the head of still another decoder in order to see how a mature knowledge of word structure (along with a mature use of context) functions in decoding unfamiliar words. Two words, <u>plentiful</u> and <u>harvest</u>, are unknown. They are in the sentence, <u>This year, farmers will have a plentiful harvest.</u>

That last word should be the name of something—maybe something that has to do with farming [syntactic and semantic

---

■ ■ **TABLE 4.8 Suffixes That Form Abstract Nouns**

Suffix	Noun	Suffix	Noun
-ness	wholeness	-hood	statehood
-ment	amazement	-ism	paganism
-ship	friendship	-dom	freedom
-ation	starvation	-ty	loyalty
-tion	deception	-ance	assistance
-ion	subjection	-ence	dependence

---

cues]. The second-to-last word describes whatever the last one is (syntactic cue). I'll work on the noun first. I wonder if e, s, t is a suffix. Probably not because e, s, t goes with adjectives and this word is a noun. There's nothing at the beginning that looks like a prefix, so probably the whole thing is a root [structural cues]. . . .

Once the reader achieves the pronunciation of harvest and recognizes its meaning, the word that describes harvest (plentiful) is semantically limited, but not to a degree that provides a direct identification. The reader, therefore, must rely on visual cues, first on those pertaining to structure. Thoughts about plentiful, then, might resemble the following.

Nothing at the beginning looks like a prefix, but f, u, l at the end looks like the suffix that means "full of." Words don't usually end in i, so the i before ful might mean that the root really ends in y. That would be p, l, e, n, t, y. Oh, plenty! Plentiful. Sure, a plentiful harvest.

Effectively demonstrated by this decoder's strategies with the two words was the combined use of contextual, structural, and graphophonic cues. And always underlying their successful use was the decoder's oral vocabulary. With oral language serving as the foundation, what was used can be graphically portrayed as follows:

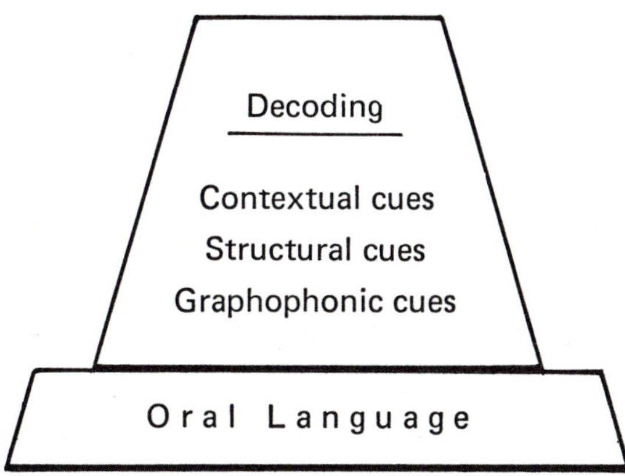

Prefixes

Once children are able to deal with commonly used inflectional suffixes and easily understood derivational suffixes, they are ready to learn about some prefixes. When prefixes do enter into instruction, teachers need to know the difference between active and absorbed prefixes, since explicit attention to the latter can confuse children about the nature of a prefix.

It is safe to predict that you are much more knowledgeable about active prefixes than about absorbed prefixes simply because the former *are* active. That is, they have a clearly apparent effect on the meaning of roots. This is shown in derivatives like unclean, disobey, reread, preschool, amoral, and antiwar. In contrast, absorbed prefixes have no semantic effect, although they once did. The lack of effect is demonstrated in words like above, defy, before, commit, admit, and absorb.

Absorbed Prefixes.   While language scholars and bright, able children may be interested in, and profit from, a knowledge of absorbed prefixes, attending to them in classrooms can introduce needless confusion. Let me illustrate this with what was seen in one third grade.

During a discussion of prefixes, the teacher wrote alone, above, and among on the board; asked a group to read them; and then explained that because the initial a in each was a prefix, the second rather than the first syllable in each word was stressed. Next she asked for additional examples of similar words. One child offered "a slide," which immediately prompted another to contribute "a rake." In response, the teacher just said, "Those are different," and switched to another topic.

Apparent in the discussion was the children's confusion about the meaning of *prefix,* perhaps fostered by the attention to an absorbed prefix. What they seemed to need was further work and practice with common *active* prefixes so that they could arrive at a clear and correct understanding of what a prefix is. Later—much later, in fact—some attention might go to absorbed prefixes, although that is not necessary. More important is that the children being instructed can automatically identify words like alone, above, and among, since they are common and are important for comprehension.

At this point you might be wondering, Why did the teacher just described call attention to an absorbed prefix? As far as I was able to tell, the only reason was that the next page in a workbook referred to it. Since that is the likely explanation, it might be time to call your attention to something that was said in the first chapter. I was urging you to study and even memorize certain material so that you will be able to "stand on your own two professional feet" and not depend on teaching manuals. I went on to say that if you are not a freer, more independent instructor as a result of studying the content of this book, it will not have achieved its central goal.

With a free, independent, knowledgeable teacher, how might

absorbed prefixes enter into instruction? Let's say that attention is going to <u>alone</u> because it is a new word. In the process, a child comments, "I thought you said that in two-syllable roots, the first syllable is stressed." "That's right," says this knowledgeable teacher. "It happens, though, that the <u>a</u> in <u>alone</u> used to be a prefix, so the rest of the word—the root—was stressed. Now, <u>a</u> isn't a prefix—the whole word is the root—but the second syllable is still stressed."

Since it is active prefixes that *must* enter into instruction, they will be discussed now.[4]

Active Prefixes. To teach active prefixes successfully, teachers have to be able to verbalize their meanings for children. Because of that requirement, see how well and easily you can put into words the meaning of some common prefixes, all of which are underlined in the derivatives listed below.

Meaning of Prefix

1. <u>im</u>mature ____________________________

2. <u>re</u>build ____________________________

3. <u>un</u>steady ____________________________

4. <u>mal</u>treat ____________________________

5. <u>anti</u>freeze ____________________________

6. <u>co</u>exist ____________________________

7. <u>post</u>graduate ____________________________

8. <u>non</u>resident ____________________________

9. <u>un</u>pack ____________________________

10. <u>under</u>pay ____________________________

[4] Possible content for more advanced work, including some with absorbed prefixes, is covered at the end of the chapter under the heading "Etymology."

When you complete your definitions, be sure to compare them with those in the Answer Key.

The prefixes that you just defined, plus others that also occur frequently, are in Table 4.9. Since they *are* common, this is the time to study any entry in the table that is not familiar. As you do your studying, keep in mind the following observations.

First, a number of commonly used prefixes mean "not." How a negative is indicated depends on how a root is spelled. If it

---

■ ■ **TABLE 4.9 Some Common Prefixes**

Prefix	*Meaning*	*Example*
in-	not	indefinite
ir-		irregular
il-		illegal
im-		immortal
		impossible
non-		nonstop
un-	not	unfair
	to do the opposite of	untie
dis-	not	disagree
	remove	disarm
under-	insufficient	underdone
post-	after	postwar
co-	together	cooperate
	joint	coheir
anti-	prevent	antiknock
	against	antiwar
counter-	against	counteract
mal-	bad, badly	malpractice
re-	again	remake
	back	recall
mis-	wrongly, badly	miscount
pre-	before	prepay

starts with r, the prefix will be ir-. If the root begins with l, the prefix is spelled il; and if the root starts with m or p, the prefix will be im-. The prefixes in-, un-, non-, and dis- are used more freely.

Also to be noted in Table 4.9 is that un- has a second meaning; namely, to do the opposite of whatever is indicated in the root. This second meaning occurs when un- is affixed to verbs (e.g., unpack, unlock, unwrap). Affixed to adjectives or adverbs, un- means "not" (e.g., uneven, unsafe, unkindly, unsuccessful). A less common prefix that also means "not" is a- (e.g., amoral, atypical).

Less frequently occurring prefixes make up Table 4.10. If any of the seven prefixes listed there are unfamiliar, this is the time to study them.

TESTING

Based on your knowledge of prefixes, please respond to the questions on page 94.

■ ■ **TABLE 4.10 Some Additional Prefixes**

Prefix	Meaning	Example
bi-	two occurring every two	bicycle biweekly
fore-	before in front	forewarn foreword
inter-	between together	interweave interlock
intra-	within	intrastate
mono-	one	monosyllable
over-	in excess	overcook
semi-	half partly coming twice	semicircle semitropical semiannual

1. What is a semiplastic purse? _______________________

____

2. How often does a semiannual sale occur? _____________

____

3. What is a horse's forelock? _____________________

____

4. If a mania is an obsession or a craze, what is a monomania?

____

5. The organization of a reading program in an elementary school may be based on interclass or intraclass groupings.

   a. What is an interclass organization? _______________

   ____

   b. What is an intraclass organization? _______________

   ____

Before proceeding, please check your answers with the Answer Key.

To sum up the discussion of some of the things that children need to know if structural cues are to assist them with decoding, let's do the exercise with regular and irregular spellings on page 95. This time:

1. Sort out the root and write it in the appropriate space. If it is multisyllabic, indicate syllable divisions.

2. Check to indicate whether the root is regularly or irregularly spelled. (A regularly spelled root, you'll recall, is one whose spelling and pronunciation match what phonic generalizations predict.)

3. In the last column provide a regular spelling for each irregularly spelled root. (Remember: one generalization is that vowel sounds in unstressed syllables are commonly reduced to the schwa sound).

REGULARLY SPELLED ROOTS?

Derived or Inflected Word	Root	Is Root Regularly Spelled? Yes	No	Regular Spelling for Root
1. overreaction				
2. ruler				
3. unemployment				
4. maltreatment				
5. threatening				
6. spongy				
7. unenviable				
8. bushes				
9. digestion				
10. unguarded				
11. curliest				
12. friendship				
13. noncancelable				
14. elbowed				
15. wonderfully				

When you have finished, check your decisions with the Answer Key.

■ ■ What Children Need to Be Able to Do to Use Structural Cues

Children who are skillful in using structural cues to decode unknown words (a) know about prefixes and suffixes; (b) know how they are pronounced; (c) know whether they add a syllable to a root; and (d) understand their effect on the meaning of roots. In addition, the children can *do* certain things. What they need to be able to do is the concern now.

Sort Out Roots

One of the things they must know how to do is what you did in the last test: sort out roots. Sorting out a root from a string of letters is important because the root may turn out to be familiar. If it isn't, sorting it out correctly allows for its being decoded correctly with the help of graphophonic cues.

Sorting out the root correctly also helps determine the meaning of the more complicated word of which it is a part. To illustrate, should <u>smiling</u> be unfamiliar, sorting out the root as being <u>smile</u> (with the help of a spelling generalization that was listed earlier) will assist not only with the pronunciation of <u>smiling</u> but also with its meaning. On the other hand, sorting out <u>smil</u> as being the root will lead to nothing but problems for both pronunciation and meaning.

The importance of sorting out roots correctly makes exercises like the following very important for children.

	Prefix	*Root*	*Suffix*
chatty	________	chat ________	y ________
trader	________	________	________
scarves	________	________	________
merrily	________	________	________
unselfish	________	________	________
intertwined	________	________	________
recaptured	________	________	________
unhappiest	________	________	________

At first, written exercises like the one above will feature inflected and derived words in which roots are known. Gradually, words with unfamiliar roots will replace them in order to allow for practice in using both structural *and* graphophonic cues. In all instances, the concern is: Now that the word is divided correctly, (a) what does it say, and (b) what does it mean?

To make practice in sorting out roots as much like real reading as is possible (and to remind children that all available cues are to be used), exercises involving contexts should not be overlooked. Once instructional time has gone to the inflection *-ly,* practice like the following is appropriate:

Root

I work puzzles <u>easily</u>. ____________

The kittens ate <u>hungrily</u> from the bowl. ____________

Everyone danced <u>happily</u> around the room. ____________

<u>Angrily</u>, the man pounded on the door. ____________

At the very beginning, the important job of sorting out roots focuses on inflected and derived words in which a root is maximally apparent because its spelling is not changed:

walking   painless   rainy   carefully

unsafe   redraw   imperfectly   miscounted

Gradually, words that are more difficult to work with because of altered spellings should enter into practice, usually in the context of other words:

funny face

icy water

digging ditches

uncaring people

incoming tide

Periodically, practice should also focus on distinguishing between what are and what are not prefixes and suffixes. Such practice will ensure that children understand the essential nature of both. If that is the goal and the prefix <u>in-</u> has been taught, contexts like the following are useful.

Root

They took the <u>indirect</u> way home. ____________

Look it up in the <u>index</u>. ____________

She is just an <u>infant</u>. ____________

An <u>inactive</u> mind is a waste. ____________

Children who grasp the true nature of word parts will understand that searching for affixes in a string of letters is essentially different from looking for little words in bigger ones. With demonstrations by a teacher, children should also be helped to see that looking for little words commonly leads to problems whether the bigger word is an inflected word, a derivative, or a root:

Problems: Seeing Little Words in Bigger Words

caring	redo	restudy	use	waste	shed	notice
car	red	rest	us	was	she	not

Thoughts of More Decoders

To see again how structural cues function with unfamiliar derived and inflected words, let's turn to the thoughts of two more decoders. The first can identify all the words except <u>im-politely</u> when she attempts to read <u>They acted impolitely in everything they said and did.</u>

It tells how they acted [syntactic cue], but people act lots of different ways [limited semantic help]. Maybe i, m is a prefix. If it is, it means "not." And l, y shows it's an adverb, so that's okay [structural help]. I don't see anything else that might be a suffix. Probably the rest is a root. Let's see. That doesn't look like any word I know. I'd better divide it. One consonant with a vowel before and after it. That makes p, o, and l, i, t, e the two syllables. Pō' līte. Pō līte'. Oh, pŭ līte.' They weren't polite. They acted impolitely in everything they said and did.

In addition to using all available sources of help in a systematic way, the decoder just described kept in mind that reading has to do with getting meaning. That is why she reread the sentence, once she had reached a conclusion about the pronunciation and meaning of <u>impolitely</u>.

The next decoder uses equally praiseworthy strategies as he works out <u>unenviable,</u> found in the sentence <u>He had the unenviable job of doing it twice.</u>

This word describes "job" [syntactic cue]. It surely is a long one. Maybe u, n is a prefix, and a, b, l, e, is a suffix [structural cues]. That leaves e, n, v, i. Not many words end in i, so I bet it's really y, not i, [spelling generalization]. E, n, v, y. Oh, envy. I know what that means [oral language]. With the prefix un, it means you don't envy him [structural help]. That makes sense [context]. I wouldn't want to have to climb into that cold water twice. He had the unenviable job of doing it twice.

If children are ever to achieve the competence reflected in the strategies of the decoders just described, teachers must keep in mind right from the beginning the three objectives of every lesson that deals with a prefix or suffix:

Objectives of Instruction

Children will be able to:
1. Pronounce whatever prefix or suffix is being taught.
2. Understand how it affects the meaning of a root.
3. Transfer what they know and understand to a new situation; that is, to an unfamiliar derived or inflected word.

Even though proficient decoders are apt to use the various kinds of cues jointly rather than successively, systematizing their use helps in the beginning. More specifically, when derived and inflected words start to appear fairly often in the materials children are expected to read, they should be encouraged to follow (with the teacher modeling the process at first) the sequence outlined below.

Consider:

1. Contextual cues
2. Structural cues
3. Graphophonic cues (if root is unknown)

Dismantle and Reassemble Word Parts

In addition to being able to sort out a root so that it can be decoded if it is not familiar, children also have to know how to put the pieces back together. By modeling the process, teachers can help children learn to use the following strategy whenever they have to work out what an inflected or a derived word says and means:

Dismantle

1. Lay aside the prefix.
2. Lay aside each suffix starting with the last one.
3. Decode the root if it is not familiar.

Reassemble

4. Put back the suffix next to the root.
5. If there is a second suffix, add that.
6. Add the prefix.

Children who adhere to the sequence when they are working with <u>unwanted,</u> <u>worthlessness,</u> and <u>insufferable</u> will lay them out (on paper at first; later, mentally) as follows:

unwanted	worthlessness	insufferable
wanted	worthless	sufferable
want	worth	suffer
wanted	worthless	sufferable
unwanted	worthlessness	insufferable

Why prefixes are added last when the parts of a word are being reassembled (and why they are removed first in the dismantling process) can be explained with the help of words like <u>unwanted,</u> <u>insufferable,</u> and <u>immeasurable.</u> Sometimes, a prefix will *not* be found attached to roots (e.g., <u>unwant,</u> <u>insuffer,</u> <u>immeasure</u>) but *will* occur affixed to derived and inflected words (<u>unwanted,</u> <u>insufferable,</u> <u>immeasurable</u>). Recognition of this indicates that the best sequence to follow for all derived and inflected words is one that removes prefixes first and adds them last.

TESTING

To make certain that you will be able to *show* children how to sort out a root and how to put the pieces back together, let's see if you can list all the steps for dismantling and reassembling the inflected and derived words shown below. The first has been done to serve as an example. (Be sure to list *every* step because, although some children will be able to skip and jump and get the job done, others have to take one small step at a time. Teachers must be prepared to help such children.) Before starting the test, it would be wise to review the six steps listed earlier and to examine the three words used to show how they are followed.

<u>unselfish</u>   <u>hopelessness</u>   <u>undersized</u>

    selfish

    self

    selfish

unselfish

<u>rekindling</u>   <u>noncancelable</u>   <u>unparadoxically</u>

Please check what you wrote with the Answer Key. Problems might indicate a need to review the six steps, the prefixes and suffixes that have been listed in various parts of the chapter, or the spelling generalizations.

■ ■ A Summary

As was pointed out in Chapter 2, English relies heavily on word order to convey meaning. That feature makes it a *positional* language.

To a lesser extent, English is also an *inflected* language. The significance of this second characteristic for meaning becomes apparent when something like <u>Your blood count</u> is compared with <u>Your blood counts</u>.

Because the forms and meanings of English words change in patterned ways by affixation, readers can use spellings to learn about the structure of unknown words. If they are inflected or derived, knowing about their structure will help a reader with both their pronunciation and their meaning.

What children need to know in order to use the structural cues that spellings provide falls under three general headings: inflectional suffixes, derivational suffixes, and prefixes. More specifically, they need to know what the affixes are; how to pronounce them; how they affect syllabication; and what effect they have on the meaning of roots.

What children need to be able to do with that knowledge can be summarized as follows:

Recognize whether an unknown word is inflected or derived
Sort out roots in derived and inflected words
Dismantle and reassemble word parts

Underlying the chapter is the contention that it is only those teachers who are thoroughly knowledgeable about word structure who can help children realize their potential as decoders. Because of the dependence of reading comprehension on correct and quick decoding, helping them realize it is no small contribution. For that reason, you are urged to reread the chapter and to restudy anything that is less familiar than it ought to be for teachers.

■ ■ Etymology

For some of you, what the chapter said about affixes simply reviewed what you knew before reading it. If that is the case, it is time to think about words in more advanced ways so that you will be ready to challenge and interest able children.

Etymology provides one way to teach more about words, since it focuses on origins, thus on word families. The rest of the chapter provides a brief look at etymology and what it offers teachers.

Classroom Observations

That etymology allows teachers to take advantage of unexpected opportunities to teach something has been verified during visits to classrooms. One observation took place in a fifth grade on the day political trials were going on in Washington, D.C. As a result of the trials, a discussion of <u>indict</u> was taking place. Questioned about its meaning, the children were able to give only vague and confused definitions. In response, the teacher commented about the many languages from which English words have come and explained that <u>indict</u> was from the Latin root <u>dicere</u>, which meant "to speak," and from the Latin prefix <u>in-</u>, whose multiple meanings included "against." She concluded, "The word indict means to 'speak against.' " The discussion that followed dwelled on the connection between that meaning and what was happening in Washington, D.C.

Subsequently, the teacher called the children's attention back to dict, reminded them that it had to do with speaking, and asked whether they could think of any word that contained the same letters. Immediately, one child proposed dictionary, eventually defined as a book of words that people use when they speak. Another child, whose mother was a secretary, added generously to the examples by offering dictate, dictation, and dictaphone, whose meanings were clarified for the other children. Writing dictator on the board, the teacher next asked why it was appropriate to call someone who ruled without asking for advice a "dictator." One child promptly explained, "What he says goes." To that the teacher added, "Yes, his word is law." And so ended an interesting and fruitful discussion of a word family.

For anyone who may think that discussions of word families must be confined to the classrooms of older children, let me describe what a third-grade teacher did on the morning a child brought a bouquet of dandelions to school. After expressing appreciation for the flowers, the teacher commented that their name was an interesting word. With everyone watching, she wrote dandelion on the board, underscoring lion. After the children identified lion, the teacher asked why a word like that would be part of a flower's name. One child said that a dandelion looked like the hair around a lion's face. The teacher praised that explanation, then wrote dent on the board. She explained that it was from a French word meaning "tooth" and that sometimes, as in dandelion, it was spelled d, a, n. The teacher underlined de in dandelion, saying it came from French, too, and meant "of." Summarizing, she called the children's attention back to dandelion, saying that it meant "tooth of a lion." She added that the flowers had been given this name by someone who thought their jagged petals looked like the jagged teeth of lions. Naturally, this resulted in growling children and, perhaps, in some who would begin to take a more active interest in words.

What was seen in a second grade also merits attention. In this case, a small group of children was being instructed in the use of a typewriter. As their teacher typed, the children eagerly watched what appeared on the paper in the machine. "What's that?" one child asked when he saw an asterisk. In response, the teacher typed asterisk, pronounced it, and said that it meant "little star." Next she typed aster, read that, and explained that it was the name of a flower that evidently had reminded someone of a star, because that was what aster meant. "Asterisk," she repeated, means 'little star.' "

Later, when I had a chance to speak to the teacher, I complimented her on her ability to discuss the meaning of <u>asterisk</u> and <u>aster</u> and inquired whether she was an expert in etymology. Laughing, she said, "Oh no. I'm just one of those crazy people who study dictionaries!" She then explained that she found it impossible to look up just one word; that, in fact, she used the need to find one word as an occasion to read about others. She mentioned, too, how pleasantly surprised she had been to find that her growing knowledge of words was highly useful, even with second graders.

Word Relationships

With all children, a teacher's knowledge of word origins and relationships fosters attention not to isolated words but to the connections that exist between them. At a beginning level, the need to teach <u>camp</u> will be seen as an opportunity to show how it relates to <u>camping</u> and <u>camper</u>. At a more advanced level, the need to teach <u>nation</u> might lead to a discussion of <u>national</u> and <u>nationality</u>. Or, at still higher levels, words like <u>cent</u>, <u>century</u>, <u>centennial</u>, <u>centipede</u>, and <u>centigrade</u> might be grouped together and defined. At another time, it might be appropriate to ask a question about possible connections between words like <u>audience</u>, <u>auditorium</u>, <u>audible</u>, <u>auditory</u>, and <u>audition</u>, or between others like <u>punctuation</u>, <u>puncture</u>, and <u>punctilious</u>.

In the classroom referred to earlier in which <u>dictaphone</u> was mentioned, the Greek word <u>phonos</u>, meaning "sound," might also have been introduced. That would have made it natural to attend to words such as <u>phonics</u> and <u>telephone</u>. In turn, <u>telephone</u> could lead to a question about the meaning of words like <u>television</u> and <u>telegraph</u>, and <u>telegraph</u> suggests still other words, like <u>autograph</u> and <u>photograph</u>. Attention to <u>graph</u> might lead to definitions for <u>autobiography</u> and <u>biography</u>, and on and on it goes. The point is: knowledgeable teachers can make the most of unexpected opportunities to teach about word structure and word meanings.

Greek and Latin Roots and Prefixes

To see what you already know about the origins of some English words, examine Tables 4.11 and 4.12. Following that,

■ ■ **TABLE 4.11 Greek and Latin Roots**

Root	Meanings	Examples
audire	to hear	audience
cedere	to move, go	precede
cyclo	circle	cycle
dicere	to speak, tell	predict
gram	something written	telegram
graph	something that records or describes	phonograph
logos	speech reason study of	monologue logic geology
mare	sea	marine
meter	measure	thermometer
mittere	to send	transmit
mobilis	movable	mobile
phobia	fear or hatred of	claustrophobia
phonos	sound	phonics
porta	door	porthole
portare	to carry	import
scire	to know	science
scope	instrument for observing	telescope
scribere	to write	postscript
sonus	sound	supersonic
spectare	to see, look at	spectacles
tenere	to hold, have	tenacious
visio	sight	vision

■ ■ **TABLE 4.12 Greek and Latin Prefixes**

Prefix	Meanings	Examples
anthropo-	man	anthropology
aqua-	water	aquarium
auto-	self, self-propelled	automatic, automobile
bi-	two	bilingual
biblio-	book, of books	bibliography
bio-	life, of living things	biology
cosmo-	world, universe	cosmopolitan
geo-	earth	geology
heter(o)-	different, other	heterogeneous
homo-	man	homocide
homos-	same, equal	homogeneous
hydro-	water, hydrogen	hydroelectric, hydrocarbon
mal-	bad, badly, wrong	malice, maltreat
micro-	small	microfilm
mono-	one, alone	monosyllable
neuro-	nervous system, of a nerve	neuritis
omni-	all, everywhere	omnipresent
per-	through	permeate, perforate
phil(o)-	love	philanthropy
photo-	light, produced by light	photograph
poly-	many	polysyllable
tele-	far off	telephone

take the time to study what you don't know. Then see how well you can do on the following test.

TESTING

Now that you have studied the content of the two tables, see what you can do with the following questions.

1. If a person was described as being a <u>bibliophile</u>, what would that tell you about him or her? ___________________

2. If a picture had to be taken with a <u>telephoto</u> lense, what would that indicate? ___________________

3. What is the difference between someone who is <u>omniscient</u> and someone who is <u>prescient</u>? ___________________

4. In a chemistry laboratory, it is likely that you would find <u>aqueous</u> solutions. What are they? ___________________

5. From its spelling, what do you suppose a <u>micrometer</u> is?

____

____

6. What is a <u>cyclometer</u>? ___________________

____

7. If a person is described as having <u>aquaphobia</u>, what does

   that reveal? _______________________________________

   ____

8. What is <u>sonorous</u> metal? ____________________________

   ____

9. Were an <u>omnibus</u> bill passed by a legislature, what kind of

   bill would it be? __________________________________

   ____

10. Is something that is <u>malodorous</u> appealing? __________

    Why (not)? _______________________________________

    ____

11. What would an <u>omnivorous</u> reader be? ______________

    ____

12. Who would be interested in having an <u>aqualung</u>? ______

    ____

Please check your answers with those in the Answer Key.

Additional Reading in Word Origins

For more work with etymology, any of the following books would be helpful and interesting.

Asimov, Isaac. *Words from the Myths*. Boston: Houghton Mifflin Co., 1961.

This book demonstrates that Greek myths, in addition to being interesting tales, are also sources of information about the origin and meaning of words and expressions in current use.

Brown, James I. *Programed Vocabulary.* Chicago: Lyons and Carnahan, 1965.

Programed Vocabulary *is just that: a study of words in a programed format that requires frequent but brief written responses. The author, a professor of Rhetoric, divides the material into studies of Greek and Latin prefixes and roots. He also offers tips for remembering meanings. Although the cover for* Programed Vocabulary *says, "For High Schools," only the specialist in etymology could describe the material as being easy or nonproductive.*

Dale, Edgar. *The Word Game: Improving Communication.* Bloomington, Ind.: The Phi Delta Kappa Educational Foundation, 1975.

This inexpensive forty-page booklet is both informative and amusing. Written by an educator long associated with vocabulary development, it offers an abundance of interesting information about words, including strategies for remembering their meanings.

Dale, Edgar; O'Rourke, Joseph; and Bamman, Henry A. *Techniques of Teaching Vocabulary.* Palo Alto, California: Field Educational Publications, 1971.

So much material is between the covers of this book that it could keep readers busy (and learning) for a long time. Techniques of Teaching Vocabulary *provides teachers with many ideas for classroom activities with middle- and upper-grade elementary school children.*

Davidson, Jessica. *Is That Mother in the Bottle?* New York: Franklin Watts, 1972.

The subtitle for this book ("Where Language Came From and Where It Is Going") explains why it is included in this list of references. The title correctly suggests that the author enjoys playing with language. The material she offers concerns word origins, especially word meanings. A reference list for further reading is included.

Epstein, Sam, and Epstein, Beryl. *The First Book of Words.* New York: Franklin Watts, 1954.

This book was written for children. Why, then, is it in a list of references for teachers? Since there is so much to learn about words and their family histories, books that deal with etymology—even those prepared for children—stand a very good chance of teaching something to all their readers. So it is with this simply written, generously illustrated publication.

Funk, Charles E. *Thereby Hangs a Tale.* New York: Harper and Brothers Publishers, 1950.

The tales told in this book are about the origins of words. Each selected word is followed by an account of how it became a part of our language and, secondly, how it came to have a given meaning.

Funk, Wilfred. *Six Weeks to Words of Power.* New York: Pocket Books, 1955.

Some of you will recognize the name Wilfred Funk as one that has long been associated with words. For many years the head of a company that published dictionaries and encyclopedias, Funk is the author of numerous books designed to help adults improve their vocabularies. Under Funk's guidance, they are likely to develop a lasting interest in words, because he works hard at making word study an enticing occupation. In Six Weeks to Words of Power, *Funk divides the study into verbs, nouns, and adjectives, covering the material in forty-two short chapters.*

Funk, Wilfred, and Lewis, Norman. *Thirty Days to a More Powerful Vocabulary* (Rev. Ed). New York: Wilfred Funk, 1975.

These authors promise their readers "a more powerful vocabulary" if they will agree to spend fifteen minutes a day on a chapter. Having made and kept the agreement, I am able to say that Funk and Lewis keep their promise with a book comprising easy-to-read, highly interesting material. Chapters have titles like "Words About Your Feelings," "Words From Classic Roots," and "Words About Doctors and Specialists."

Greenfeld, Howard. *Sumer Is Icumen In.* New York: Crown Publishers, 1978.

How English has changed and developed over the centuries is the theme of this book. The author even makes some predictions about English in the future.

Klein, Ernest. *A Comprehensive Etymological Dictionary of the English Language.* New York: Elsevier Publishing Co., 1971.

Anyone who is curious about the origin of a particular word can learn about it in this dictionary, which divides into Volumes I (A–K) and II (L–Z). To interest children in etymology, teachers might also use this dictionary to learn about the origin and meaning of the children's names.

Kraske, Robert. *The Story of the Dictionary.* New York: Harcourt Brace Jovanovich, 1975.

While explaining how dictionaries for adults and children come into existence, Kraske tells about word origins. When he describes how dictionaries are updated, he also deals with how and why word meanings change.

Laird, Helene, and Laird, Charlton. *The Tree of Language.* Cleveland: William Collins & World Publishing Co., 1977.

Approximately half of this book tells "Word Stories." Prior to these accounts, chapters bear titles like "The Beginning of English," "English Spelling and How It Got That Way," and "Names and How They Began."

Morris, William, *It's Easy to Increase Your Vocabulary* (Rev. Ed.) New York: Penguin Books, 1975.

"Behind almost every one of our everyday expressions there exists an intriguing story." So says William Morris, who used intriguing tales to write It's Easy to Increase Your Vocabulary. *Morris is editor-in-chief of* The American Heritage Dictionary.

Nurnberg, Maxwell, and Rosenblum, Morris. *How to Build a Better Vocabulary.* New York: Popular Library, 1977.

Written by two professors, this inexpensive paperback has twenty-four chapters with titles like "Every Word Has a History," "Do You Read the Sports Page?" and "Something to Remember Them By." For any who are unsure of either the pronunciation or the meaning of foreign words and expressions (e.g., carte blanche), *the two chapters called "Translation, Please" offer assistance. Like so many other paperbacks that deal with vocabulary development, this one includes periodic opportunities for self-testing.*

O'Rourke, Joseph P. *Toward a Science of Vocabulary Development.* The Hague, Netherlands: Mouton and Company, 1974.

A little more difficult than other books in this list, Toward a Science of Vocabulary Development *provides an academic study of meanings and relationships, as well as practical ideas for helping middle- and upper-grade children with vocabulary.*

Sorel, Nancy C. *Word People.* New York: American Heritage Press, 1970.

Some words derived from specific people. For instance, quisling, meaning "traitor," originated with a Norwegian named Quisling, who betrayed his country during World War II. And the sandwiches you eat are named for an English Earl of Sandwich. Word People *tells the stories of eighty-three words and the people who account for them.*

A SYNTHESIS

Cueing System of English

Progression in Teaching about Cues

Successful Instructional Programs

Ideally, children would know every word in whatever they had to read or wanted to read. Since the ideal is hardly common, they need to be ready to figure out what any important but unknown word says and, therefore, means. What can be taught to enable children to do that without the assistance of another person or a dictionary has been the central concern of this book. Because four kinds of cues make independent word-identification ability possible, classroom instruction and this book focus on them.

■ ■ Cueing System of English

The four types of cues that provide help with word identifications stem from certain characteristics of English. To begin, it is a positional language, which establishes syntactic cues. Like all other languages it makes sense, and that brings semantic cues into existence. That it is an inflected language accounts for structural cues, and graphophonic cues are available because an alphabetical writing system records English.

■ ■ Progression in Teaching about Cues

Classroom attention to cues can and should begin even before children start to read, because syntactic and semantic cues are available in spoken as well as written language. In neither spoken nor written English, however, can the two kinds of cues be counted on to identify words directly. Instead, they contribute by placing grammatical and semantic constraints on what any given word in a given context can be. They function, then, by narrowing down possibilities.

Spellings—even incomplete spellings—narrow down possibilities still more. Since letters stand for speech sounds, a knowledgeable use of letter-sound relationships contributes directly and substantially to correct conclusions about an unfamiliar word's pronunciation.

Acquainting children with letter-sound relationships, also

referred to as graphophonic cues, is the purpose of phonics. Since the syllable is the unit of pronunciation, phonics also covers syllabication. More specifically, it teaches children how to use visual cues (letters and their sequence) to divide unknown words into syllables. Once divided, they are ready to be decoded with the help of generalizations that focus on letter-sound relationships and the factors that affect them.

Because only visual cues are available when a word is unfamiliar, everything done in phonics must concentrate on them. What *is* done should enable children to learn on their own what a root says. If the root is familiar in its spoken form, knowing what it says will signal what it means. This close relationship between spoken language and the successful use of cues explains why all teachers should feel a special responsibility to do everything possible to extend oral language abilities.

Once children begin to encounter inflected and derived words in print, they need to learn how to use spellings for a second purpose: to identify affixes so that roots will be sorted out in the process. In turn, determining what the root is will assist with the pronunciation and the meaning of the more complex word.

The amount of a decoder's attention that each type of cue merits depends on the word that is causing problems and on the context in which it is embedded. At first, when almost all words are roots, structural cues play an insignificant role in decoding, whereas graphophonic cues are of central importance. Later, as inflected and derived words become common, the importance of structural cues for both pronunciation and meaning increases noticeably. Meanwhile, graphophonic cues continue to be useful with unknown roots.

If the amount of help offered by a context is generous, other cues should serve only to confirm or question what the context indicates the word is. On the other hand, when contextual help is meager, spellings—and, with them, graphophonic and structural cues—assume great importance.

Essentially, the decoder's job is to get a word figured out both correctly and quickly; and that requires a balanced use of all available cues. To foster the use of them all, practice in applying what has been taught should concentrate on unknown words that are in a context. Within the framework of running prose, children will come to see that all that is required is an approximately correct pronunciation, since that will trigger the correct one—*assuming* the word is in their oral vocabularies.

Even with able decoders, too much preoccupation with a word may obscure the meaning of the sentence in which it is found. That is why teachers should encourage children to reread a sentence once a troublesome word has been decoded. Periodic reminders to do that reinforces the fact that the reason for decoding a word has to do with communication.

■ ■ Successful Instructional Programs

Programs that stand a chance of turning out skillful decoders allot sufficient time for both instruction and practice. What is necessary is portrayed below.

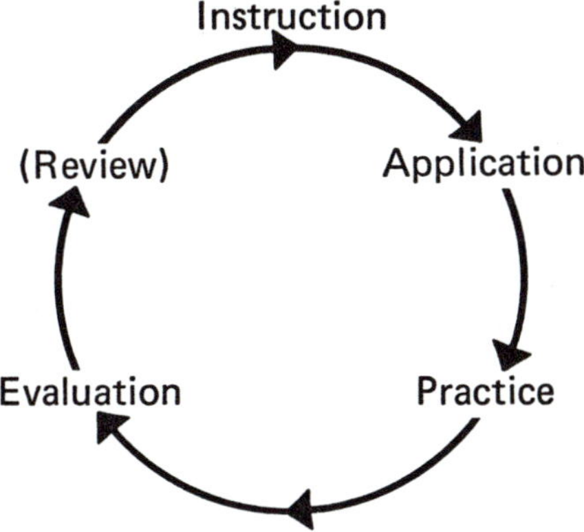

Teaching Decoding Skills

What the diagram suggests is a cycle that goes as follows. Instruction focuses on a clearly defined objective. For instance, children will learn a certain phonic generalization. Once they seem to understand it with the help of known words, they are shown how it works with new words. This is the application stage of the lesson, when the teacher supervises efforts to use what was taught. It is a critical part because it demonstrates to children the practical value of knowing about generalizations. Next comes practice, a time when children try to use what was taught (again with new words) without a teacher's help. What they are or are not able to do on their own allows for evaluation. The evaluation, in turn, helps a teacher decide whether more of the same is needed, or whether something else can be introduced.

And so it is that children gradually accumulate the understandings and skills required for proficient decoding. The thrust behind *Strategies for Identifying Words* is the fact that such ability will evolve only when those who instruct children are themselves thoroughly knowledgeable about decoding.

 Appendix

GENERALIZATIONS

1. For Dividing Words into Syllables

(A) Inflected and Derived Words

Most affixes are syllables. For instance:

untie   spotless   passes

The inflection -ed adds a syllable when affixed to a verb ending in d or t. Otherwise it just adds /d/ or /t/. For instance:

needed   rooted   stayed   asked

When ion is affixed to a root ending in /t/, the letters tion compose the last syllable. For instance:

action   perfection   creation

(B) Roots

When two consonants are preceded and followed by vowels, a syllabic division generally occurs between the consonants. For instance:

album   al bum

When vowels precede and follow a consonant, a syllabic division generally occurs between the consonant and the preceding vowel. For instance:

coma   co ma

When x is preceded and followed by vowels, the preceding vowel and x are in the same syllable. For instance:

axis   ax is

When a root ends with a consonant followed by le, the three letters compose the last syllable. For instance:

spindle   spin dle

Vowel and consonant digraphs function as if they were single letters. For instance:

pauper   pau per   siphon   si phon

2. For Vowel Sounds

When a syllable has one vowel and it is not in final position, the vowel generally stands for its short sound. For instance:

pen   index

When a syllable has one vowel and it is in final position, it generally stands for its long sound. For instance:

she   silo

When a syllable has two successive vowels that are not special digraphs, the long sound of the first is common. For instance:

bead   aim

When a syllable has two vowels, one of which is a final _e_, and the two are separated by a consonant, the long sound of the first vowel is common. For instance:

tape   pile

When a syllable has two vowels, one of which is a final _e_, and the two are separated by two consonants, the short sound of the first vowel is common. For instance:

since   edge

The digraph _oo_ has long and short sounds. For instance:

cool   cook

The digraph _ow_ stands for a diphthong and for the long _o_ sound. For instance:

owl   own

When a vowel is followed by _r_ in a syllable, one of three _r_-controlled sounds is common. For instance:

her   car   for

3. For Y Functioning as a Vowel

When _y_ is in medial position in a syllable that has no vowel, it usually stands for the short _i_ sound. For instance:

gym   symbol

When <u>y</u> records the final sound in a multisyllabic word, it usually stands for the long <u>e</u> sound. For instance:

sorry   autopsy

Otherwise, <u>y</u> usually stands for the long <u>i</u> sound. For instance:

typhoon   asylum

---

4. For Schwa Sound

Vowel sounds in unstressed syllables are commonly reduced to the schwa sound. For instance:

pil<u>o</u>t   <u>a</u>way   church<u>e</u>s

---

5. For Consonant Sounds

When <u>c</u> and <u>g</u> are followed in a syllable by <u>e</u>, <u>i</u>, or <u>y</u>, they generally stand for their soft sounds. Otherwise, the hard sounds are common. For instance:

cent   gem   call   tag

Together, <u>q</u> and <u>u</u> stand for either /kw/ or /k/. For instance:

inquire   baroque

The letter <u>x</u> can stand for /ks/, /gz/, or /z/. For instance:

Texas   exam   xerox

The digraph <u>th</u> records a voiced and a voiceless sound. For instance:

them   thimble

B Appendix

GLOSSARY

Absorbed prefix.   One or more letters that once functioned as an active prefix but no longer do.

Active prefix.   One or more letters placed before a root to alter its meaning.

Affix.   A term that refers to a prefix or a suffix.

Alphabetic writing system.   A way of recording words that relates their symbols to their pronunciations.

Base.   The member of a word family with the simplest structure.

Blend.   A synthesis of speech sounds.

Cluster.   Two or three consonants that often occur as adjacent letters in syllables, each of which stands for a sound.

Compound word.   A word composed of two or three roots.

Connected text.   Two or more running words that convey something meaningful.

Consonant.   In phonics, refers to all the letters except a, e, i, o, and u.

Context.   A series of related words that may be less or more than a sentence.

Contextual cue.   The help with an unknown pronunciation or meaning that derives from known words appearing in the same context.

Cue.   A prompt, or hint, about an appropriate response.

Decoding.   Using a written word's spelling to achieve its identification.

Derivational suffix.   One or more letters added to the end of a root to alter its meaning.

Derivative.   A word composed of a root and a prefix; a root and a derivational suffix; or a root, a prefix, and a derivational suffix.

Derived word.   A word composed of a root and a prefix; a root and a derivational suffix; or a root, a prefix, and a derivational suffix.

Digraph.   A pair of vowels or consonants that stands for a sound that is unlike the sound associated with either letter making up the pair.

Diphthong.   A close blend of two vowel sounds.

Etymology.   A study of the origin of words.

General context.   The written selection in which a given word appears.

Grapheme.   A linguistic term for "letter."

Graphemic base.   A series of letters beginning with a vowel that often constitutes part of a syllable or word.

Graphophonic cue.   The help with a written word's pronunciation that stems from the connection between letters and speech sounds.

Hard sound.   Traditionally used in phonics to refer to the sounds recorded by <u>c</u> and <u>g</u> in <u>call</u> and <u>go</u>.

Homonym.   A word that has diverse meanings, depending on the context in which it occurs.

Inflected language.   One in which the forms and meanings of words are changed by affixes.

Inflected word.   A word composed of a root and an inflection.

Inflection.   One or more letters added to the end of a root to alter its grammatical function.

Inflectional suffix.   One or more letters added to the end of a root to alter its grammatical function.

Listening vocabulary.   All the words a person understands when they are used orally by others.

Local context.   The words that constitute the phrase or sentence in which a given word appears.

Long vowel sound.   In phonics, the vowel sounds in <u>aim</u>, <u>eel</u>, <u>ice</u>, <u>old</u>, <u>use</u>, and <u>pool</u> are called "long."

Marker.   One or more letters or a word that signals information about other letters or words.

Noun marker.   A word in a given context that indicates a noun will occur either immediately or eventually.

Oral vocabulary.   All the words that are known to an individual in their spoken form.

Phoneme.   A synonym for "speech sound."

Phonic analysis.   Examination of an unknown word to see what its spelling suggests for its pronunciation.

Phonics.   A body of content about connections between letters and speech sounds designed to help children figure out the pronunciation of words that are unknown in their written form.

Phonogram. A series of letters beginning with a vowel that often constitutes part of a syllable or word.

Positional language. One in which word order determines meaning.

Prefix. One or more letters placed before a root to affect its meaning.

Regularly spelled word. One whose pronunciation can be predicted from the generalizations taught in phonics.

Root. The member of a word family with the most simple structure.

Schwa sound. An unstressed, deemphasized sound closely resembling the short sound for u. It appears commonly in unstressed syllables and is symbolized by ə.

Semantic cue. The help with an unknown word that derives from the meaning of known words in the same context.

Sentence. A series of words that are ordered in a way that produces meaning.

Short vowel sound. In phonics, the vowel sounds in and, end, if, odd, us, and book are called "short."

Sight vocabulary. All the written words that an individual can identify instantaneously.

Soft sound. Traditionally used in phonics to refer to the sounds recorded by c and g in cent and gem.

Speaking vocabulary. All the words a person can pronounce and understand well enough to use them correctly in speech.

Stop sounds. Consonant sounds that are noticeably distorted when an attempt is made to produce them outside the context of a syllable.

Structural analysis. Examination of an unknown word to see if it is a root or an inflected or derived word.

Structural cue. The help with the pronunciation and meaning of an unknown derived or inflected word that is found in letters that record affixes.

Suffix. One or more letters added to the end of a root to affect its meaning or grammatical function.

Syllable. A vowel sound that is usually combined with one or more consonant sounds.

Syntactic cue. The help with an unknown word that establishes its grammatical function based on its placement in a given context.

Syntax. The structure of a sentence established by its word order.

Tense marker. One or more letters affixed to the end of a verb that indicate its tense.

Vowel. In phonics, refers to the letters a, e, i, o, and u.

Word family. A group of related words whose roots are either identical or of the same origin.

Appendix

REFERENCES

1. Brown, Roger. *Words and Things.* New York: The Free Press, 1958.

2. Deighton, Lee C. *Vocabulary Development in the Classroom.* New York: Teachers College Press, Columbia University, 1959.

3. Durkin, Dolores. *Phonics, Linguistics, and Reading.* New York: Teachers College Press, Columbia University, 1972.

4. Durkin, Dolores. *Teaching Them to Read.* 3rd ed. Boston: Allyn and Bacon, 1978.

5. Durkin, Dolores. *Teaching Young Children to Read.* 3rd ed. Boston: Allyn and Bacon, 1980.

D Appendix

ANSWER KEY

Page 6

1. *Graphophonic cues* are the hints about a word's pronunciation that are found in its spelling. (Such hints exist because in an alphabetic writing system, letters stand for sounds.)

2. *Structural cues,* or hints, are also rooted in spellings, this time helping a reader learn whether the unfamiliar word is a root alone or a root joined with one or more affixes. (*Affix* is a general term that refers to a prefix, a suffix, or an inflection.)

3. *Contextual cues* are the hints about a word's identity that come from known words in the same passage.

4. A *cue* is the help with an identification that comes from the spelling of the unknown word and from the known words that are in the same context.

Page 7

An *alphabetic writing* system is one in which words are recorded on the basis of their pronunciation. In such a system, letters stand for speech sounds.

■ ■ **CHAPTER 2: Use of Context to Identify Words**

Page 10

1. A *general context* is the selection in which an unfamiliar word occurs. It might be a story, a newspaper article, or a set of directions for making something.

2. A *local context* is the particular sentence in which the unfamiliar word is located.

Page 12

1. A *positional language* is one in which the order, or sequence, of words determines meaning. (Even brief con-

nected text like *a day off* and *an off day* reveal the significance of order for meaning.)

2. A *syntactic cue* is the hint about a word's identity that derives from its placement in a phrase or sentence, thus from its relationship to other words in the same context.

Page 13

2. preposition   5. conjunction   8. article, pronoun, or possessive noun

3. adjective   6. verb

4. adjective   7. adverb

Page 14

1. tire   3. black   5. stairs

2. umbrella   4. daughter

Page 14

A *semantic cue* is the help with an identification that comes from the meaning of the words that a reader is able to identify. (Because of their meaning, only certain words make sense.)

Page 16

Readers' knowledge about a topic and the vocabulary that goes with it (background knowledge, oral vocabulary) facilitates correct predictions about the identity of unfamiliar words appearing in a selection on that topic (general context). For example, readers who know about jogging and its effects would suspect that *breath* is the word omitted from the context, "Now he's out of _____________. He jogged too much." Support for the correctness of *breath* comes from the meaning of the available words (semantic cue). Still more comes from the construction of the sentence (syntactic cue), which calls for a noun at the place where the word is omitted.

Page 25

1. positional	5. plural	9. combined (or correct)
2. meaning	6. noun	10. unknown (or unfamiliar)
3. syntax	7. semantic	11. eliminated (or omitted)
4. syntactic	8. maximum	12. spelling (or letters)

If any of your responses are different from those shown above, ask yourself, Does my answer *make sense?* If it does, it is correct. Remember: making sense is also at the heart of contextual practice carried on with children.

■ ■ CHAPTER 3:   Use of Phonics to Identify Words

Page 30

A child's *oral vocabulary* is made up of all the words the child knows in their spoken form. (Oral vocabularies divide into listening vocabulary and speaking vocabulary. A child's listening vocabulary is composed of all the words he or she understands when they are used by another. Less sizable is the speaking vocabulary: the words the child knows well enough to use them in his or her own speech.)

Page 30

The easiest words for readers to figure out with graphophonic cues are those that are known in their spoken form. This is so for several reasons. One is that a context offers maximum help with an identification when the unknown word is familiar orally. Specifically, if children know about salt and pepper, a context like Pass the salt and pepper will be very helpful should <u>salt</u> be unknown visually. Also to be remembered is that if children work out the pronunciation of <u>salt</u> by using graphophonic cues, they will have no way of knowing whether it is correct if <u>salt</u> is unknown orally as well as visually. Finally, the approximately correct pronunciations that often result from the use of graphophonic cues are most easily changed to precisely correct ones when the word in question is in the reader's oral vocabulary. In summary, oral vocabularies provide readers with important prompts for identifying words. They also allow for a response to the question, Does this word make sense?

Page 37

The column labeled "Letters" should have *cluster, digraph, grapheme, graphemic base,* and *phonogram.* The terms *blend, diphthong,* and *phoneme* belong under "Sounds."

Page 37

1. *Decoding* is using the spelling of a word to learn what its pronunciation is.

2. A *cluster* is two (or three) consonants that often appear successively in a syllable. It stands for two (or three) sounds.

3. A *blend* is a combination or synthesis of sounds.

4. A *digraph* is two letters (vowels or consonants) that stand for a single sound that is different from the sound associated with either letter.

5. A *phonogram* is a pronounceable unit that is spelled with a vowel followed by one or more consonants. Often, it constitutes part of a syllable.

Page 38

1. A blend is the synthesis of two or more sounds. Since it is impossible to draw a circle around sounds, it is impossible to "circle all the blends."

2. A digraph is not a sound. It is two letters (vowels or consonants) that stand for one sound.

3. Sounds cannot be seen. A correctly worded question is, "What letter do you see at the end of <u>plant</u>?" Another correctly stated question is, "What sound do you hear at the end of <u>plant</u>?"

To sum up, all three statements fail to distinguish between terms that refer to letters and terms that refer to sounds.

Page 40

sig nal   tab let   chim ney   mon soon   suc cess

Page 40

When two consonants are between two vowels, a syllabic division generally occurs between the consonants.

Page 42

1. baple	2. ento	3. gixas	4. honat
durcle	idfer	uxot	nefut
rinfle	thoftan		phanitt
			sticess

1. When a word ends in a consonant followed by <u>le</u>, those three letters constitute a syllable.

2. When two consonants are preceded and followed by vowels, a syllable division generally occurs between the consonants.

3. When <u>x</u> is preceded and followed by vowels, the preceding vowel and <u>x</u> are in one syllable while the vowel that follows <u>x</u> is in another syllable.

4. When a single consonant is preceded and followed by vowels, the preceding vowel is in one syllable while the consonant and the vowel that follows it are in another syllable.

Page 42

Omission: The two consonants must also be followed by a vowel; otherwise, no letter is available to record the necessary vowel sound. According to the incorrect generalization, a word like <u>sent</u> divides into <u>sen</u> and <u>t</u>, which is impossible, since every syllable must have a vowel sound.

Page 43

Error: Not one of the examples has /b/ in medial position, a fact made apparent when the words are divided into syllables: <u>num ber</u>, <u>ga ble</u>, <u>al bum</u>, <u>sym bol</u>.

Page 43

It is useless because if <u>spider</u> is unfamiliar, a reader won't know what sound <u>i</u> stands for. If he or she did, there would be no reason to divide spider into syllables. A generalization like this one turns syllabication into an end in itself when, in fact, it should be a means for getting *unknown* words decoded.

Page 47

cellophane   array   nomad   synthesize   maintain

typhoon   condone   trophy   emblem   blaspheme

As these markings point up, the schwa sound is very common but does not occur in *every* multisyllabic word.

Page 50

Voiced Sound	Voiceless Sound
there	thing
them	with
those	thumb
that	

Page 51

beet	tell	fault	stress
3 phonemes	3 phonemes	4 phonemes	5 phonemes

pun	thin	guess	shine
3 phonemes	3 phonemes	3 phonemes	3 phonemes

tax	brook
4 phonemes	4 phonemes

Page 51

1. *Words with Consonant Clusters*

broom	gasp	stood
clean	glance	
dust	prince	

2. *Words with Consonant Digraphs*

bathe	king	shame
chop	mouth	thug
cinch	phase	

3. *Words with Short Vowel Sounds*

chop	foot	prince
cinch	gasp	stood
dust	glance	thug
elm	king	

4. *Words with Long Vowel Sounds*

bathe	phase
broom	pool
clean	seed
gaze	shame

5. *Words with Soft Sound of C*

cinch	prince
glance	

6. *Words with Hard Sound of G*

gasp	glance
gaze	thug

Page 54

1. <u>dreack</u>
Two adjacent vowels that are not special digraphs generally stand for the long sound of the first one.

2. <u>crodix</u> (cro-dix)
   (a) A single final vowel usually stands for its long sound.
   (b) A single vowel that is not in final position generally stands for its short sound.

3. <u>stadge</u>
When a vowel and a final <u>e</u> are separated by two consonants, the likely sound is the short sound of the first vowel.

4. <u>thade</u>
When a vowel and final <u>e</u> are separated by one consonant, the likely sound is the long sound of the first vowel.

Page 58

1. bur ro yes (in first syllable)
2. ur chin yes
3. spi ral no
4. a ro ma no
5. sor row yes (in first syllable)

Page 59

1. t ype Not possible.
2. s ymbol Not possible.

    3. m yrtle   Not possible.
    4. law yer   Possible.
    5. fanc y   Not possible.

Page 60

    1. type   (Silent *e* indicates one syllable.)
    2. sym bol   (Spelling pattern: VC CV)
    3. myr tle   (Consonant plus *le* is a syllable.)
    4. fan cy   (Spelling pattern: VC CV)

Page 60

    1. type   *Long i sound*
    2. symbol   *Short i sound*
    3. myrtle   *R-controlled*
    4. fancy   *Long e sound*

Page 61

    1. slon ny   2
    2. bray no   3
    3. slym   1
    4. pry ple   4
    5. slyte   4
    6. oy ton   oy: special digraph as in *oyster*

Page 63

	Hard Sound	*Soft Sound*
1. angry	X	
2. splice		X
3. success	X	X
4. gentle		X
5. emerge		X

Page 64

		Yes	No	Regular Spelling
1.	trauma (trau ma)	X		
2.	buffalo (buf fa lo)	X		
3.	once (once)		X	wunce
4.	sauce (sauce)	X		
5.	textile (tex tile)	X		
6.	torpedo (tor pe do)	X		
7.	urge (urge)	X		
8.	wolf (wolf)		X	woolf
9.	thread (thread)		X	thred
10.	gargle (gar gle)	X		
11.	finance (fi nance)	X		
12.	vaccine (vac cine)		X	vaccene
13.	mourn (mourn)		X	morn
14.	among (a mong)		X	amung
15.	volcano (vol ca no)	X		
16.	flood (flood)		X	flud
17.	accent (ac cent)	X		
18.	sympathy (sym pa thy)	X		

Page 73

church	ĭlk	cŭff	pawn	ēach	cūbe̸
ur	ĭ	ŭ	aw	ea̸	ū
chur	ĭl	cŭ	paw	ēach	cū
church	ĭlk	cŭff	pawn		cūbe̸

■ ■ **CHAPTER 4: Use of Structural Analysis to Identify Words**

Page 79

1. True.
2. False. The two kinds are derivational and inflectional.

3. False. Two roots can be found in the spelling of <u>notice</u> and <u>carpet</u> (<u>not</u>, <u>ice</u>; <u>car</u>, <u>pet</u>), but neither is a compound word. With compounds, the pronunciation of the roots is maintained, and there is a semantic relationship between them. The compound <u>pancake</u>, for example, refers to a cake that is made in a pan.

4. False. Such words have a phonic, not a semantic, relationship. Unfortunately, some commercially prepared phonics materials erroneously refer to words like these as a family.

5. True. All derive from the Latin infinitive <u>dicere</u>, which means "to speak." A dictionary is a list of words used in speech. Dictation refers to a written account of what someone says. Indict means to speak against someone. And a dictator is one whose word is law.

6. True.

7. True. This statement was included to make the point that classifying some words is not as easy as the definitions might suggest. In <u>ceaselessly</u>, <u>less</u> is a derivational suffix, which suggests it is a derived word. On the other hand, <u>ly</u> is an inflection, which indicates it is an inflected word. The answer, then, is that <u>ceaselessly</u> is an inflected derivative. More important for children than being able to classify <u>ceaselessly</u> is knowing that <u>cease</u> is the root; that <u>less</u> affects its meaning; and that <u>ly</u> affects it grammatical function.

Page 80

ly (7, 9)	drawbridge (10)	maltreat (5, 8)
barrels (3)	ment (1)	il (6)
star (2, 4)	mice (3)*	nameless (5, 8)

Page 83

1. When a singular root ends in <u>f</u>, the plural form is made by changing the <u>f</u> to <u>v</u> and adding <u>es</u>.

2. When a root ends with a consonant that is preceded by a

---

* Like <u>barrels</u>, <u>mice</u> is an inflected word, since it is a plural. Unlike <u>barrels</u>, it does not adhere to the customary way of showing plurals

single vowel, the consonant is doubled before ed, er, ing, or y is added.

3. When a root ends in a silent e, the e is usually dropped whenever a suffix that starts with a vowel is added.

4. When a root ends in a consonant followed by y, the y is changed to i before a suffix is added.

Page 91

1.	immature	not
2.	rebuild	again
3.	unsteady	not
4.	maltreat	badly
5.	antifreeze	prevent
6.	coexist	together
7.	postgraduate	after
8.	nonresident	not
9.	unpack	to do the opposite of
10.	underpay	insufficient

Page 93

1. semiplastic: partly plastic
2. semiannual: twice a year
3. forelock: hair in front that hangs down toward the eyes
4. monomania: excessive concern or enthusiasm for one thing
5. interclass: children from different classrooms are grouped on the basis of abilities or problems

   intraclass: children in a single classroom are grouped

Page 95

Root	Is Root Regularly Spelled? Yes No		Regular Spelling for Root
1. act	X		
2. rule		X	rool

Root	Is Root Regularly Spelled?		Regular Spelling for Root
	Yes	No	
3. em ploy	X		
4. treat	X		
5. threat		X	thret
6. sponge		X	spunge
7. en vy	X		
8. bush		X	boosh
9. di gest	X		
10. guard	X		
11. curl	X		
12. friend		X	frend
13. can cel	X		
14. el bow	X		
15. won der		X	wunder

Page 100

hopelessness	undersized	rekindling
hopeless	sized	kindling
hope	size	kindle
hopeless	sized	kindling
hopelessness	undersized	rekindling

noncancelable	unparadoxically
cancelable	paradoxically
cancel	paradoxical
cancelable	paradox
noncancelable	paradoxical
	paradoxically
	unparadoxically

Page 107

1. A <u>bibliophile</u> is a lover (phile) of books (biblio).

2. A <u>telephoto</u> lens is used to photograph (photo) an object that is distant (tele).

3. An <u>omniscient</u> person knows (scient) all things (omni). One who is <u>prescient</u> has the power to know (scient) before-hand (pre).

4. An <u>aqueous</u> solution is a water (aqua) solution.

5. A <u>micrometer</u> is a measuring instrument (meter) for something small (micro); for example, distances and angles.

6. A <u>cyclometer</u> measures (meter) the rotations of a wheel (cyclo) in order to ascertain distance traveled.

7. <u>Aquaphobia</u> refers to fear (phobia) of water (aqua).

8. The word <u>sonorous</u> describes metals that produce a sound (sonor) when tapped.

9. An <u>omnibus</u> bill covers many (omni) things.

10. No, what is <u>malodorous</u> is not appealing because it smells (odor) bad (mal).

11. An <u>omnivorous</u> reader reads (devours) everything (omni).

12. Divers would want an <u>aqualung</u> because it allows them to breathe (lung) underwater (aqua).

INDEX